MIKO

PA FLIGHT 120 LOS ANGELES–LONDON 7.41 AM | WESTMINSTER BRIDGE 3.45 PM | LU FLIGHT 037 LONDON–FRANKFURT 6.31 PM

HORST WACKERBARTH

A DAY IN THE LIFE OF LONDON

Jonathan Cape Thirty Bedford Square London

JONATHAN CAPE LTD, 30 BEDFORD SQUARE, LONDON WC1B 3EL

First published 1984
Designed and produced for Jonathan Cape Limited
by J.M. McGregor Pty Ltd PO Box 40 Double Bay NSW 2028 Australia
Copyright © J.M. McGregor Pty Ltd

ISBN 0 224 02975 4

PROJECT DIRECTOR:	**MALCOLM McGREGOR**
PROJECT ORGANISERS:	**RED SAUNDERS AND SYD SHELTON**

EDITOR:	**MALCOLM McGREGOR**
DESIGN AND ART DIRECTION:	**SYD SHELTON**
PICTURE EDITORS:	**BRUCE BERNARD AND ANDY DARK**
CAPTIONS:	**DON ATYEO**
INTRODUCTION:	**DAVID WIDGERY**
DESIGN ASSOCIATES:	**RED SAUNDERS, RUTH GREGORY AND ROGER HUDDLE**
EDITORIAL CONSULTANT:	**MICHAEL RAND (SUNDAY TIMES, LONDON)**

RESEARCH:	**SUE READY AND BILL HAYES**
PROJECT ASSISTANTS:	**PHILIP LORCA DICORCIA (USA)**
	WILL WHITE AND TOBY GLANVILLE

PHOTOGRAPHIC CONSULTANTS:	**JENNIFER CRANDALL (ESQUIRE, NEW YORK)**
	SUE DAVIES (PHOTOGRAPHERS GALLERY, LONDON)
	ALICE GEORGE (TIME/LIFE, NEW YORK)
	LAURIE KRATOCHVIL (ROLLING STONE, NEW YORK)
	PATRICIA STRUTHERS (MAGNUM, PARIS)

BLACK AND WHITE PRINTS:	**FTP, LONDON**
E6 COLOUR PROCESSING:	**CETA, LONDON**
ORIGINATION:	**REGENCY, SYDNEY**
BROMIDES:	**PADPRINT, SYDNEY AND JO'S BASEMENT, LONDON**
TYPESETTING:	**THE TYPOGRAPHERS, SYDNEY**
PRINTING:	**THE POT STILL PRESS, SYDNEY**
BINDING:	**BOOK GRAPHICS, MELBOURNE**

PHOTOGRAPHIC EQUIPMENT:	**KEITH JOHNSON PHOTOGRAPHY, LONDON**
SPECIALIST CAMERA EQUIPMENT:	**CANON AND NIKON**
BLACK AND WHITE MATERIALS:	**ILFORD**

SYD SHELTON

MALCOLM McGREGOR

RED SAUNDERS

Wednesday, September 14, 1983, dawned over wet pavements in the world's largest metropolis. Crisp winds and heavy showers, alternating with chill glaring sunlight, brought out the coats and umbrellas abandoned throughout the long hot summer. London was putting on its most vigorous climatic display for the one hundred photographers who had been judiciously selected and assembled to record life as it is lived in the 610 square miles that comprise the capital of Britain. It was to be a midnight-to-midnight vigil, taking a frantic six weeks of meticulous organisation requiring no fewer than 37 languages and untold tons of gear. The result, it was confidently predicted, would be an entirely fresh and unexpected view, a taking of the visual pulse, of the most photographed society on earth: one day in the life of London.

The idea was conceived by London photographers, **Syd Shelton** and **Red Saunders**, and Australian based publisher **Malcolm McGregor**, who had together just completed work on *A Day in the Life of New Zealand*. The London project turned out to be an altogether more exacting exercise. In the wild chaos of a single large room in Soho, the portfolios of legendary, eminent and hitherto unknown photographers from all over the world were sifted, while those chosen were matched with locations involving hours of wheedling on the telephone for permission to enter prisons, zoos, television studios, control towers, monasteries, Turkish baths, operating theatres, tube tunnels after the last train has passed, and even the sewers. This last produced one of the most unwelcome adventures when Peter Lavery dropped his entire box of equipment into the torrent of murk through which he was wading chest-deep. There was no alternative but to dive to retrieve it, before his next engagement with the chef at the Waldorf Hotel.

The photographers themselves were as varied in outlook, style and technique as the city they were to portray. Andre Kertesz was the eldest at 89, and eight automatic Canon cameras were pressed into the hands of children, to see what would happen. Distinguished veteran war photographers, advertising people, political photojournalists, paparazzi and Polaroid portraitists made up the team of one hundred, supplemented by a score of local photographers who, caught up in the enthusiasm, submitted their pictures on spec. In all, 100,000 shots of more than two thousand locations were collected, developed, pored over and sifted down to the three hundred selected for this book.

For the first time ever in one volume, the full range of photographic techniques is shown at its best in an unprecedented study of a microcosm of the Western world at work and play. From the grainy 35 mm black-and-white of Don McCullin, Mike Abrahams and Pennie Smith to the ultra-grain of the new low-light, super-fast colour films of John Claridge, so beautifully enhancing the air of decay in dockland; from the naturalistic full-colour Kodachrome of Chris Schwartz and doyen William Klein to the filtered artistry of the advertising plate cameras of Ken Griffiths, Denis Waugh and Christine Hanscomb; from the 20-second-exposure panoramas of Laurie Lewis to the manipulated SX70 ballet-scenes of Joe Partridge — they are all shown here in an extraordinary kaleidoscope.

But techniques are merely a means to an end and often life gets in the way. Barbara Billingham had her car towed away while she photographed traffic in the City; Neil Selkirk was requested by the management to remove his clothes if he wanted to take photographs in the Turkish bath. As Red Saunders shouted to one of the journalists above the pandemonium of the Soho office which also served as equipment store, hot-line telephone exchange, all-night canteen and camera repair workshop: "We're going to blow away all this video garbage and re-establish the primacy of real photography, of images."

The eye is constantly beguiled through the pages of this book. Strippers in Fulham pubs, car workers under the watchful eye of a suspicious management, the dying in a Hackney hospice, the living in the Stock Exchange and on the streets of the East End — all play their part in this extraordinary manifestation of the heart of London in the 1980s, felt so keenly by inhabitants and visitors

London began as a garrison port at the extremity of someone else's empire — two hills, a bridge and some timber quays overlooking an unappetising salt estuary. With its curious climate, rich soil and godless citizens, it attracted both mercenaries and missionaries to become the epicentre of the biggest empire since the Roman, the place whose adaptable and wildly expressive Mercian dialect, once printed and made presentable, has become the *lingua franca* of the modern world. The city where the political theories of labour and capital were first minted originated as little more than a bend in the river, a place shallow enough to ford safely and deep enough to harbour merchant galleys and troop ships.

If inferior in status, practical geography guaranteed its importance. Londinium was the junction point of the great, straight roads the Romans sliced across their conquered country and the most convenient port for troop reinforcements but when the centurions returned to Rome for good, the city quickly reverted to its unruly natives and was once again, like nineteenth century Africa, divided and fought over by rival missionaries and quarrelling traders. Even for them, London proved hard to conquer or convert. The Pope's ambassadors were sent packing to Canterbury and the men who called themselves Kings of England stayed a safe distance away at Winchester. So if London had an international reputation by the early Middle Ages, it was the unruly one of a free trade area — a Shanghai or Tangier — where merchants from the developed world could trade profitably with the semi-civilised inhabitants of the far North. It was because the Thames emerges where the route from Constantinople and Venice via Amsterdam encounters the North Sea, that Bede singled London out as '. . . a mart town of many nations which repaired thither by sea and land' and its identity was shaped through commerce and communication rather than as a royal seat or centre of religion.

Recognising this in 1066, William the Conquerer did not raze the city but offered it autonomy if it would acknowledge his succession, and built his palace at Westminster, a diplomatic distance away from the self-governing city whose walls had been rebuilt along the Roman plan. William's tower (of white Normandy limestone) overlooked — and was meant to overawe — a city which was already overspilling its compact fortifications. By Tudor times, London had become a straggling, seaside town whose watercourse was its main street, main drain and main medium of communication.

The land axes of modern London begin here too. The great princes built their palaces along the strand between the City and Westminster. The lawyers indicted and then evicted the order of Knights Templar to establish their professional headquarters which still stretch from Gray's Inn at Holborn to the Inner Temple on the river. Henry VIII's avaricious anti-Papism enabled the annexation of the monastic lands which became first the royal hunting grounds and then the sequence of great parks which guarantee London's leafy, open centre. As in so many London matters, 'freedom' had cash and land at the root of it.

It was still a dirty, ramshackle and disorganised town which, not for the first or last time, went up in smoke in 1666. But if London's position as the most westerly great city of Europe made it the last recipient of the Renaissance, we owe to that delay the superb self-confidence of Christopher Wren, a mathematician turned architect and town planner, who transformed London from a wooden town to a city of brick and stone and steeples. Wren's complete rebuilding plans (like Abercrombie's post-Blitz design) were blocked by the intricate patchwork of land owned by merchants too greedy to be grand. If modern sight lines are ruined by office buildings of unrelieved banality, it is still possible to glimpse Wren's dream by extrapolating the lines of his and Hawksmoor's City churches (financed as a Christian counter-insurgency campaign in stone) to the pinnacle of St Paul's, that most homely of cathedrals, whose prodigious dome is the most successful flouting of planning permission ever.

As residential London pressed its chessboard of squares and terraces west, John Nash mapped out the great curves which still define the West End. The sweep from Regent's Park to St James's is a grand conception but one can also appreciate the cockney in its classicism which bolted together terraces as robustly as a bathroom plumber. Above all it is the Victorian city, its chief period of construction and population growth, that we inherit today. It was Victorian ambition and ingenuity which indented East London with her colossal docks (an ugly Venice with nearly seventy miles of berthspace); burrowed and blasted the railway lines which terminate in those majestic stations which make the approach by rail so auspicious; rammed hygienic roads through the rookeries; transplanted cemeteries, expanded the parks, threw up baronial breweries, grim police stations, imperious board schools, forbidding hospitals, made abbeys out of gas works, turned water towers into turrets and frothed up fandangles for its bridges.

Here the giants are men like Joseph Bazalgette, engineer-architect of the Embankment, Hammersmith Bridge, Battersea Bridge and the Beckton outfall sewer and Brunel the Elder who devised the tunnelling shield which drove the way for the London Underground — men to whom the only adequate tribute is the modern Thames Barrier. Eighteenth-century London architecture was highly innovative. The New Road (1756) along the northern edge of central London was the world's first bypass, the Adelphi (1768) the original housing estate and Somerset House (1776) a pioneering office block. However, it was the Victorians who made modern London. Beside their achievement, Edwardian erections such as the Bank of England facade, the Admiralty Arch and Kingsway are mere dentistry. The work of the modernists, whose best achievement is the Royal Festival Hall and worst can conveniently be seen on either side of it, seems curiously conservative by comparision.

The density of history when combined with the impossible size of the metropolis is easily overwhelming. So Londoners retreat to a village (or two) of their own which make habitable and workable what would otherwise be an inert and uninhabitable sprawl. Some of the geographical villages like industrial Woolwich, once rural Enfield, Saxon Pinner or thirteenth-century Highgate were independent hamlets engulfed by the remorseless expansion of the city's borders. Other more modern congregations within the Green Belt's girdle established their identity between the wars, when London's built-up area tripled to establish the Metroland of the commuter suburbs.

It is above all the tube trains' extensive northern network and the railways' southern junctions which make possible the dreadful compression of 60% of office space into central London — a mere 2% of London's land area — and which shoe-horns in the twice daily surge tides of over a million commuters. However the famous map of the Underground system, although a beautifully organised graphic, is an unreliable piece of cartography, as one finds when trying to match it with the A–Z street plan. If Greenwich Observatory begins the world at London, Beck, London Transport's designer, begins London at Hampstead.

Metroland, as viewed by the passing motorist, is a demoralising sequence of mock-Tudor facades glaring over privet hedges but, on investigation, often reveals its own delicate internal structure. Ham, Syon, Osterly and Chiswick have grown up around great mansions, Fulham and Hampton Court have their palaces and neurotic Islington, chaste Hampstead Garden Suburb, utopian Bedford Park and Dutch-Jacobean De Beauvoir Town are all, in their quite different ways, coherent designs for metropolitan villages. Suburbanisation has its own status system according to altitude, with the middle class wedges fanning out over the hill villages and workers living close to the industries. Although council house quality is uneven, its existence has prevented the wholesale eviction of working class people from the city centres to satellite estates devoid of any of that sense of neighbourhood which is the urban dweller's most precious asset. And there is much variety and not a little distinction in London's public

housing; in the half-mile East of Shoreditch Church one sees styles ranging from Derbyshire's nineteenth-century work for Baroness Burdett-Coutt's Metropolitan Association for Improving the Dwellings of the Industrial Classes through to Denis Lasdun's fifties' cluster-blocks for the London County Council and contemporary low-rise, high density developments.

Hampstead sits smugly above London like an Austrian burg. Its air of labyrinthine insularity arose from its geographical position but has become part of its personality. For all its alleged radicalism, it is as unchanging as a country churchyard. Earls Court, however, radiates such an air of rapid transit it is almost an extension of the airport lounge. Richmond, for all its pretended langour, has a melodramatic landscape and bloody history — it was at Turnham Green that the London-trained bands stemmed the Cavalier assault on London in the Civil War — whereas Mayfair, once grand and witty, is now a most tedious place, a bad impersonation of Olde English refinement. Bloomsbury's once intimate squares were annihilated by the ugliest university in the universe, making it anathema to the aesthetes to which it was once home.

However it is Greenwich which remains the pearl of the suburban villages. Its architecture is as regular and uplifting as Handel, its art gallery sublime and its intrepid boats, dry-docked but still tearing at their concrete moorings, the best reminder of London's maritime traditions. It is impossible not to be moved by the rakish hull of the Cutty Sark which brought first tea from China and then wool from Australia in record times or by the tinyness of the Gypsy Moth in which Francis Chichester, solo, circumnavigated the globe. Approaching Greenwich, whether by ferry from Westminster or through the lugubrious tunnel from the Isle of Dogs (where the royal hounds were once boarded out of noble earshot) is always an adventure. To view London for a moment as a yokel, from the summit of the steep hills of Greenwich Park, while the skateboarders swoop downwards, is to find an even more satisfying vantage point than that among the kite flyers on the crest of Parliament Hill Fields. For all its grandness, Greenwich is pleasingly unpretentious. It is entirely the right place for the Western Hemisphere to commence.

There are occupational villages which keep hours as strict and particular as pubs. Fleet Street, where the daily press that Londoners read in such quantities is written and printed, lies, appropriately enough, over an ancient sewer. Echoing all day (it, not St Paul's, possesses the real whispering gallery) even the most bibulous journalists have been decanted away by mid-evening, relinquishing it to the night printers and the drivers of those lethal newspaper lorries which hurtle from the presses to the main rail terminals. Legal London lurks in its cloistered courtyards and 5,000 people mill about in the Palace of Westminster imagining they run the country. Dagenham, the gigantic Ford Motor Company car plant, is another world of its own which used to boast of taking steel and coal and rubber in at one end and driving finished automobiles out at the other. It almost seems to throb as you approach it, as do 20,000 round-the-clock workers who converge on the factory from all over south-east England every day and whose shop stewards despair of uniting a work force which supports 26 different football teams.

The most exclusive village of all is that of London-by-night. There is a wordless camaraderie shared by the invisible workers who staff the night emergency services, guard, inspect and repair the moving parts of the city and clean and renew it for another day's light. At the night cafes and early morning coffee stalls, cooks, cleaners, musicians, prostitutes and even police share a paternalistic puzzlement over their now sleeping charges and hold in common the nocturnal knowledge of quite how casually the big city is capable of taking life and hope away.

As one of the oldest ports in maritime history, London has always been a global village. Over the past twenty years, one third of new Londoners have come from overseas — 130 mother tongues are spoken in London schools. So besides the Angles, Saxons, Jutes, Celts, Vikings, Danes and their offspring came the French Huguenots, the Irish forced from their own land by famine, the longstanding Italian settlement in Clerkenwell, the Chinese outpost in Limehouse and the refugees from the terrible anti-Semitic purges of the Tzarist autocracy who built the classic Jewish ghetto in Whitechapel. In the twentieth century migrants from central and Mediterranean Europe were joined in the post-war, labour-hungry period by black Londoners from the Caribbean, North Africa and Asia in an almost exact process of imperialism-in-reverse. (One of the most succinct slogans of migrants' defence organisations has been 'We are here because you were there'.)

There is a very definite London-Jamaican or London-Irish identity and rampacked in a Brixton dancehall or at the Southall Horse Fair, it is felt almost more intensely than in Kingston or Connemara. There are some quite separate national villages, almost walled gardens, containing Thai monasteries or Polish monarchists or Nigerian political emigres (although all, including the saffron monks, have learned to sport an umbrella), but what is generally remarkable is how well Londoners of all shades have dealt with the unpredictable sequence of post-war events which have made our city a testing ground for a modern, multiracial cosmopolitanism. There are rich rewards for this modern mix and the

illuminating challenge it offers to the identity of the English Establishment and island joy-in-gloom mentality. It is characteristic of ordinary Londoners' instinct towards kindliness that even at the height of racist agitation, opinion polls found that people who were against 'immigration' in the abstract, didn't dislike immigrants at all and objected very strongly to the Fascist Right.

For there is now, especially in the classrooms, sports-grounds and streets, much more successful interconnection and cross-fertilisation than many moralists appreciate. Brick Lane, for example, usually seen as the heartland of the Bangladeshi migration and the site of the Great Mosque whose building previously served the Jewish and Huguenot faiths, is, in its intimate mix-up of manufacture, dwelling and leisure, very far from a ghetto with a wide racial mix speaking in Cockney, Gujarati and Yiddish. This mix produces such London anomalies as the Tory Sikh devoted to the monarchy and the video, the St Lucian who sustains the NHS and the Bible, the Turkish-Cypriot Elvis clone, the turbanned stationmaster and the white Londoner rated 'well hard' in even the most testing reggae DJ clashes.

Another aspect of the same concerned tolerance makes London a mecca for subcultural stylists. London street style is intricate and depends for its effect on a visually discerning audience. It is part of the London love affair with fancy dress, part of the dandyism which has been going on in London streets for centuries. The current style magazines are the exact equivalent of seventeenth-century guides to sophisticated deportment and their adherents require of their fellow citizens not just to be tolerated but to be appraised. Londoners are never rude (except intentionally).

The sheer joy and pleasure of being an inhabitant of this great city is the birthright of all Londoners. It is the right to watch working ships shoulder their way through the fortified dock walls onto the river. It is the finding of new challenges for old London skills (for if our city is beautiful and civilised it is to the degree that it has been a working place not just a residential shell). It is the right to be frivolous and to be taken by bus No. 22 to World's End, without the conductor raising an eyebrow, via the Bank and Balls Pond Road (where the publican Ball used to let patrons shoot the ducks on his pond) along routes once used by milkmaids and coaches and four. It is to run over Primrose Hill (no primroses but alive with the sound of plimsolls), to break the ice on the Serpentine to swim on Christmas Day, to row for the Doggett's Coat and Badge and rush the imperial frontage of Wembley Stadium as rebels might overwhelm New Delhi. It is to eat pizza in Oscar Wilde's favourite restaurant, curry in the shadow of Hawksmoor, capuccino in Old Compton Street and cooked breakfast in the stable of Kenwood House. It is to hear ragas in the Purcell Room, dub plates in the marble and brass of Fulham Town Hall music-hall under a pneumatic bubble theatre in Highbury Fields and Elgar set to brass from a deck chair in Hyde Park. It is to rally against apartheid between the paws of the imperial lions in Trafalgar Square, to lay seige to the last prison built on Panopticon lines to free the Pentonville Five (the London dockers briefly locked up in 1972) and it is to spout at Speakers Corner, Tower Hill and their equivalents on the corners of London's multitudinous street markets. It is to smell and hear something in the air that could only be this city; the cinnamon and brine wind that blows down Wapping High Street, the aromatic damp of the Kew Palm House, the sweetness of hops and cumin seed in Brick Lane, the glue and diesel breeze which announces the south exit of the Blackwall Tunnel, the Sunday felicitations in Gerrard Street and the particular clatter as the Household Cavalry cross from gravel to roadway at Hyde Park Corner.

What true Londoner has not experienced the catch in the throat when bounding up the stairs of the British Museum with its wonderfully pagan sodium lighting, when hurrying across Hungerford Foot Bridge as the sun sets over willowy Waterloo Bridge — the feeling that makes booting a football across just one of the 386 acres of Hampstead Heath a lyrical and slightly savage experience.

London's spirit remains elusive and has a reputation of defeating the artist who seeks to plunder its surface beauties without comprehending its personality. It is a city better drawn (above all by Hogarth) than painted, even when painted by Monet, Pissarro or that great Cockney landscapist J.M.W. Turner. Its pungent language and odd characters have best suited picaresque novelists, from Fielding to MacInnes. It is caught better in fragments of observation rather than any grand epic, which is why Dickens and Johnson are such enduring and perennially illuminating observers; and why the city, though written to death and regularly stripped of its mysteries, remains such an undying and magical subject.

This book has succeeded in a way that those who set the project in motion, can hardly have imagined possible. For it has caught the elusive personality of a vast and various city and done so with affection but quite without sentimentality. The combined effect of so many pairs of eyes wringing meaning out of 24 hours of city life sets up a process which is more akin to animation than simply montage or juxtaposition. Flicking back and forward, characteristics, outlooks and expressions suggested in one photograph recur, alter and interact. There is a refusal of the expected and a willingness to express emotions towards the inhabitants of the city shared by the photographers and clearly reciprocated by their subjects.

One photographer was asked, "Shouldn't you be out taking pictures of London?" Replying, "You are London", he was told, "Well, I just live here, but how about the buses or Tower Bridge or something?" It is because the book is about her and people like her rather than the buses and the Tower, that it reveals the city so well and catches it in an acutely self-conscious moment. But London in the early eighties is facing a complicated crisis in its own identity which goes far beyond the fiercely contested proposal to abolish the Greater London Council, which would render it the only capital in Western Europe without an elected authority. The levels of unemployment displayed on ghastly chronometers outside inner London town halls mark an end of the period when the docks and engineering defined London's industrial personality. Our photogenic red buses are threatened not just by juggernauts and jams but a funding crisis in the whole of London's public transport. While the city is alive with ingenious reconstruction, public building in the rest of London has halted as the river is further walled up by a procession of office blocks. The scale of these changes is huge. The architectural historian sees the rebuilding of Docklands and Bankside as a bigger scheme than Wren's; the economist sees the industrial changes required as more fundamental than the 1930s or even the 1890s; the educator, artist and hospital administrator alike, face fundamental changes.

Paradoxically, this very uncertainty is acting to sharpen Londoners' civic sense and historical imagination. The partisan enthusiasm with which Londoners welcomed, encouraged and egged the Day In The Life of London photographers, who had their city on loan for 24 hours, is an aspect of that feeling. In return we have been given a vision of the city we take so for granted which will surprise and excite even the most knowledgeable citizen.

One cockney couple caught sight of a participating cameraman who was photographing a car dump from high on a tower block in East London. Their first reaction was pride that a feature of their own area should provoke such interest. Then, with the sun setting over St Paul's dome, they returned and showed him another view from the same spot and said quietly, "That's London too." Most Londoners want their city both ways: the glossy mythologies and the grainy black and white, the dreaming spires and the car wreckers, the patrician past and the socialist future, the labour ward and the hospice, the aristocracy and Jimmy, King of Clerkenwell, the Governor of the Bank of England and the guv'nor of the Progressive Working Man's Cafe, the oysters and the fish and chips. Now we have it, in a remarkable photographic achievement which enables us to see properly Dr Johnson's 'wonderful immensity' for the first time.

UNDERCOVER WORK

Looking like a couple of Arab oil sheiks in their protective clothing, two London Transport cleaners take a break from their all-night shift cleaning the underground. London Transport employs approximately three dozen men to clean the underground networks. While some tunnels require constant attention, others are visited only once or twice a year. Either way it's a chokingly dirty job.

15

WEDNESDAY MORNING FEVER 1 AM

Gravel-throated disc-jockey Gary Crowley's 'Tuesday Club' at Bogarts in South Harrow attracts 400 committed dancers every Tuesday night. 'It's the ultimate night out,' croaks Crowley. 'If you don't dance, don't come.'

Following page: Underneath the Arches: 2.30 am: Cold, damp and a cardboard mattress — the grim reality of a night under Charing Cross arches for London's burgeoning homeless. Up to 150 homeless of all ages doss down under the railway bridges by the Embankment each evening. With fewer and fewer hostel beds available and more unemployed arriving in London in search of work, the number increases every day.

20

EMILY ANDERSEN

THE LAST WALTZ   4.30 AM

Left: The music has finally stopped in 'Heaven', the London disco most famous for its 'gay' nights, leaving one last lone couple swaying to the sounds of silence.

Above: While other clubs have long since given up the ghost, 'Slum It With Style' night at the Camden Palace hammers on into the small hours. One thousand-plus of London's trendiest night-clubbers, in various states of attire ranging from the sublime to the very ridiculous, conspire to pack the cavernous former theatre each evening, making the Palace the hottest nightspot in town and its patron, Steve Strange, a media star.

22

TIM O'SULLIVAN

I WALK THE LINE

Left: London Transport maintenance team H-Gang during their 4½ hour shift repairing the tunnels and track of the underground network. The work, all heavy labouring, can only be done after the stations have shut down for the night.

Above: A lone patrolman arrives at Leicester Square tube station during his night's walk along the Picadilly line. The job, surely one of the loneliest in London, requires patrolmen to walk alone clearing obstacles and litter from the tracks. Between them LT's patrolmen walk the entire underground network — all 250 miles of it.

THE WORK   6.15 AM

Casual labourers in Camden Town wait to be driven to Brighton for a day's building work. At precisely 6 am the men — almost exclusively Irish — gather by the hundreds in the streets behind Camden Town tube station, anxious for a day's work allegedly without the trouble of tax returns and national insurance stamps — cash in hand, no questions asked. Photographer Gill Galvin: ''Suddenly they're just there, hundreds of them, standing in groups, crouched in doorways in the dark. At ten past six the vans appear to ferry them all over the country. Some of the men climb in immediately, others wait to be selected. They all know what's going on, but when I asked questions they swore at me and turned their backs. Twenty minutes later it's like it had never happened: the vans are gone, and those men left simply vanish.''

JOHN LONDEI

MEAT OFF THE HOOF

Meat porters Gerry Branch, John Hibbert, Gil Gorbell and Bill Stephenson have already been shouldering carcasses and dodging barrows for several hours at Smithfield wholesale meat market in the heart of London. There has been a meat market at Smithfields in some form or another since the twelfth century, when Thomas à Becket's clerk recorded 'a smooth field where every Friday there is a celebrated rendezvous of fine horses to be sold, and in another quarter are placed vendibles of the peasant, swine with their deep flanks, and cows and oxen of immense bulk.' Since then the cobbles have run with blood, not all of it animal. During the sixteenth century Smithfields became the place of public executions; in 1558, more than 200 persons were burned at the stake for their religious beliefs.

Left: Simon removes the first loaves of the morning from the ovens at Hampton's Bakery.

ONCE MORE AROUND THE PARK   6.30 AM

At 6.30 am the horses and riders of the Household Cavalry have Rotten Row in Hyde Park to themselves — save for the occasional Rolls-Royce returning home to Mayfair.

Previous page: Two small arrivals from Nigeria waiting wearily in the transit lounge of Heathrow's Terminal 3 for an onward flight to New York.

THE CAVALRY

Members of the Household Cavalry mount up for their day's ceremonial duties.

JOHN BULMER

32

TV BREAKFAST 6.55 AM

Five minutes before TV AM goes on the air, presenters Mick Owen (left) and John Stapleton (right) are grateful for any outside distractions to ease the tension — even if it's just another camera.

WHOLE LOTTA BULL

John Causon, head herdsman of the Wrotham Park Estate in the London borough of Barnet, with his pride and joy, three-year-old Wrotham Shining Excalibur. Wrotham Park, just 13 miles from the city centre, is the largest working farm in the London metropolitan area. Its 2,300 acres of arable land support, among other things, 200 jersey dairy cows — and Wrotham Shining Excalibur, owned by Mr Julian Byng. Already the father of four calves, he enjoys the honour of having had his semen frozen and stored by the Milk Marketing Board for future use.

A horse grazes on Mudchute Farm on the Isle of Dogs, one of a handful of inner-city farms in London. Mudchute, built on 30 acres of mud dredged from the bottom of the Thames during the construction of Millwall Docks, is the result of a campaign begun in the late 1970s by local groups to save the area from becoming part of the general decay of the surrounding docklands. Today, Mudchute is the home of horses, donkeys, goats, sheep, cows, rabbits, chickens, geese, ducks and bees. It makes its own honey and its own yogurt, both of which are sold at a farm shop. It also attracts visitors from all over the city — especially children, anxious to try their hand at horse riding. Indeed, without children Mudchute would find it difficult to continue; each evening local schoolchildren arrive to lend a hand with the day-to-day running of the place.

CHRIS MOYSE

BENEATH THE CITY STREETS

Mile End Road tube station, and the morning rush into the city is at its peak. One and three-quarter million Londoners make the journey underground every day.

Previous page: Pripan Singh arrives home from his job on the Heathrow Airport night shift in time to have breakfast with his sons, Gurginder and Ajip, before they leave for school. The Singhs, who came to Britain 16 years ago, live in Southall's Golf Links Estate where they, together with other Asian families living on the estate, are the target of a continuous campaign of racial harassment. Their house has been stoned. When Pripan's wife, Rashan, goes shopping, youths try to snatch her bags. Once, a bottle of urine was hurled through their front door. The two boys do not play outside because they are frightened of being attacked by the gangs of skinheads who prowl the estate. The family desperately wants to move.

FOOD FOR THOUGHT   8.40 AM

'Progressive Working Man's Caterer' reads the sign on the window of the Quality Chop House in Farrington Road (left), and for 42 years owner/chef Eddy Enricho has been living up to the promise in the form of gargantuan breakfasts — as did his father before him. Eddy's day begins long before the 6 am opening time when he arrives to prepare the pies and pastries. His first customers are night-shift workers and up-all-night revellers, followed by a succession of cloth cap working men, Fleet Street reporters, City gents and, finally, young trendies attracted by the biggest breakfast in town — kippers, porridge, toast, bacon and eggs.

Fresh kippers (above) from the new Billingsgate fish market, still the home of fresh fish in London despite a recent, and controversial, relocation.

CHRIS MOYSE

THE DAILY GRIND   8.55 AM

Right: Commuters wait at East Croydon Station for the 8.57 to London Bridge.

Above: Descending on a West End escalator.

Previous page: The new £520 million flood gate at Woolwich — the world's largest movable flood barrier — gleams against the backdrop of the city it protects. The Thames Flood Barrier consists of ten gates in all. When raised they stand more than 52 feet — the height of a five-storey building — above the river bed, giving London an additional seven feet of protection against surge tides. 'There was last night the greatest tide that ever was remembered in England to have been in this River, all Whitehall having been drowned,' wrote Samuel Pepys in his diary for 7 December, 1633. London's engineers hope that the Thames Flood Barrier will prevent a recurrence.

STEPPING OUT

Left: Bond Street, the most exclusive shopping thoroughfare in London.

Above: The last of the morning's commuters trickle out of St Pancras station.

A DEATH IN THE FAMILY

The coffin of a 14-year-old
boy leaves a Chelsea
funeral parlour for burial.

Previous page:
Commuters cross the road
outside Victoria Station
on their way to work.

53

COLIN STILL

SUBURBAN TEMPLES

Above: September 14 was a day of special celebration for the adherents of the Krishna Consciousness Movement — it was the anniversary of the appearance on Earth of the Goddess Radha, consort of Lord Krishna. Rising at 3 am, the devotees spent most of their long day chanting and dancing ecstatically in the Radha Krishna Temple in Soho Square. After an eight-hour puja, or prayer meeting, during which time they observed a strict fast, the disciples then tucked into a 160-course vegetarian banquet.

Right: Buddhist monks from Thailand meditate in the Buddhapadipa temple in Wimbledon, the heart of the London stockbroker belt. The temple has been in this unlikely setting for six years and houses a permanent staff of six monks, plus a floating population of visitors.

55

ROYAL NAVAL HOSPITAL, GREENWICH

The Royal Naval Hospital at Greenwich, photographed from the Isle of Dogs. Completed in 1705, the building was the combined work of Vanbrugh, Hawksmoor and Sir Christopher Wren, and provided accommodation for 2,000 Royal Navy pensioners. It also displays on the ceiling of the main dining room in Wren's adjoining Naval College, the finest example of baroque painting in the country — a vast allegorical painting by James Thornhill depicting *The Triumph of Peace and Liberty*. To the right is the last — and most famous — of the clipper ships, the *Cutty Sark*, now permanently moored at Greenwich.

Previous page: All 400 places in the taxi 'feeder' park at Heathrow air terminal are full. For the queuing drivers it means a long, unpaid wait, yet Heathrow remains London's most popular rank for cabbies — at the very least there's a £15 fare into town, plus there's always the chance of that £100 trip to Birmingham.

Previous page: Sewer men Rodney Faversham (left) and Johnny Burgess at their place of work. The assignment was not Lavery's favourite. After shooting for almost three hours in the miles of winding Victorian tunnels, he knocked all his exposed film into three feet of raw sewage. ''I was in it — literally — up to my neck. I was pretty uncomfortable for the rest of the day. Unfortunately my next assignment was the head chef at the Waldorf, cooking crepes Suzette.'' This photograph is one of the few which survived the dunking.

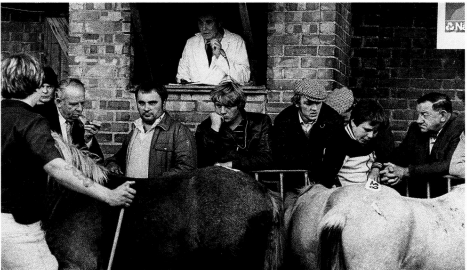

HORSE TRADING

Horse traders examine the merchandise at the Wednesday horse fair in Southall. The fair, which has been running since 1691, is the bargain basement of horse trading, providing animals for as little as £5. (An exception to the dubious quality of most of the horses led around the ring was the white stallion pictured; it fetched £700.) Many of the customers are rag and bone men.

In recent years the fair has changed dramatically after pressure from animal welfare groups to close it down. Now there are stalls for the horses and barriers separate buyers from livestock.

64

CLEAN SWEEP 9.45 AM

Above: Lee Gillary, a London cabbie for 28 years, pilots his taxi through the Hampstead Road car wash.

Left: Bus stop near Green Park station, Picadilly.

Following page: The *B.P. Rapid* and its cargo of 700 tons — 210,000 gallons — of premium-grade petrol docks at the B.P. terminal at Fulham. The *Rapid* is an 'estuarial craft' — a fancy name for a river boat. It is used solely for transferring petroleum from one terminal to another along the river. Because of the enormous tidal changes on the Thames, the *Rapid* can only reach the Fulham terminal once every 12 hours, at high tide. The petroleum boats are among only a handful of survivors from a once flourishing riverboat trade now all but killed off by road transport.

ALL IN THE FAMILY

Royal lookalikes Gladys Crosbie (Queen Mother), Peter Hugo (Prince Charles) and Paula Dene (Princess Diana) break for an un-regal lunch in Holland Park. All three have been professional royal doubles with the Ugly Modelling Agency for the past two years, addressing banquets, opening fetes and generally performing the duties of their royal counterparts. All began their careers when they noticed the number of total strangers remarking on their resemblance to royalty, a resemblance so striking it sometimes even bemuses the lookalikes themselves.

Right: A coach-load of Japanese tourists takes it in turns to have themselves photographed beside the guard at the side entrance of St James's Palace.

JOHN BENTON-HARRIS

WIL WHITE

EYES IN THE SKY   10 AM

Left: A helicopter follows the course of the Thames — the only helicopter route allowed over the city.

Right: Brian Wolfe, Capital Radio's Flying Eye, usually sorts out London's rush hour snarl-ups from the window of his Cessna. Today, however, the low cloud has grounded him, much to his frustration.

UP AND DOWN

Railings reflected in the Serpentine, Hyde Park's lake.

Right: The 52 floors of the National Westminster Tower, the tallest building in London and the second tallest in Europe, soar imposingly into the morning sky.

READ ALL ABOUT IT

Above left: John Mead, picture editor of the *Daily Express*, displays the first prize in the *Express*'s Gold Card Bingo — a cheque for £1 million. Almost overnight Fleet Street found itself in the throes of a bingo 'war', with papers vying with each other to offer the biggest prize. So far, nobody had won the *Express*'s million — or any of the other millions being thrown about. Circulations, however, had soared.

Above right: Rain, hail or shine most London homes have their newspapers delivered.

Left: Londoners are noted for preserving their anonymity behind a newspaper.

76

The staff — and customer — of eel and pie sellers M. Manze in Tower Bridge Road, Bermondsey, take time out before the lunchtime rush. Once as ubiquitous as McDonald's, London's eel and pie shops, with their menu of jellied eels, displayed live in the window to guarantee freshness, meat pies and green 'liquor' sauce, provided the working classes with cheap dietary staples. Now less than a handful remain, mostly family businesses like this one.

SANDRA LOUSADA

SANDRA LOUSADA

LITTLE LINGUISTS   10.05 AM

Above: Morning story time at Hatfield Infant and Nursery School in Porchester Gardens mesmerises children of all nationalities. Founded in 1954.

Right: Pupils at the Bousfield Junior Mixed and Infants School, South Bolton Gardens, Earls Court.

Following page, left: Shoe shop, Brick Lane.

Following page, right: Fred Collins' hardware store in Earlham Street. Founded almost a century and a half ago by a member of the Collins family, its daunting interior is a chaos of ancient and overflowing stock, stacked it would appear, at random. After 56 years behind the counter, however, Fred Collins knows precisely where to find each item.

SENIOR SERVICE

Nora Curtin has been cooking and cleaning for gentlemen in the same exclusive Pall Mall club for 14½ years. Her working day begins at 7 a.m. when she leaves the upstairs servants' quarters and begins preparing breakfast in the kitchens below. It ends at 7.30 p.m. "Yes, I suppose you could say they're long hours, but you have to work for your bread, don't you."

Previous page: Concorde, the pinnacle of British engineering, glides out of its hangar and taxis across the perimeter road surrounding Heathrow Airport on its way to take-off. When Concorde crosses the road, all lesser forms of transport stop — some for longer periods than others.

TOWERS OF POWER 10.30 AM

Battersea Power Station, monument to a past era of industrial glory, looms imposingly on the Thames south bank. Built in 1933, the generating station exploded the belief that an industrial building had to be ugly. Since then it has become one of London's most famous landmarks, celebrated on posters, post cards and record sleeves. Now, with its working life at an end, a dinosaur on the electricity generating grid, its future hangs very much in the balance, although the threat of demolition would appear to have been averted following a popular outcry. Recently the Central Electricity Generating Board has sponsored a £100,000 competition to find a new use for its decaying industrial cathedral.

JOHN STURROCK

LOCKS AND STRIKES

Angry workers picket Britain's toy factory in Walthamstow during a dispute over compulsory overtime. The workers, objecting to having to work a 50-hour week, walked out on July 29. After an eight-week strike they returned, having won a 49-hour working week, but suffering a reduction in pay.

Right: Brick Lane, and an orthodox Jewish shopkeeper hurriedly unlocks his establishment obviously still with the fear of molestment in his mind.

89

WILLIAM KLEIN

GONE WEST

Late summer tourists and shoppers in the West End.

Previous page: Terence Kichenside, overseer of mammals at London Zoo, with one of the Zoo's llamas.

93

OLD SOLDIERS NEVER DIE

Second World War veteran Mr R. House, photographed
beside the war memorial on the Fulham Road. Mr House, a
member of the 5th Battalion — The Buffs — which served
in North Africa, lost both his legs outside Tunis in 1943.

Above: Second reveille wakes the King's Troop in their
St John's Wood barracks. A 100-year-old ceremonial
regiment, the Troop is responsible for firing the guns on the
Queen's birthday.

JEREMY NICHOLL

THE FACE THAT LAUNCHED AN OIL RIG   11.15 AM

Right: Prime Minister Margaret Thatcher arrives at Britannic House for the inauguration of a new BP oil production platform, the Magnus. Developed at a cost of £1.3 billion, the Magnus weighs 70,000 tons, is three times the height of Big Ben and, according to its designers, is capable of withstanding 100-foot waves and 100-mile-an-hour winds. It will need to be; the Magnus is sited 125 miles north-east of the Shetland Isles at the farthest tip of Europe's most northerly oil field.

Above: Social Democratic Party candidate Sara Moncur canvasses eleventh hour support on the eve of next day's council elections. There are three by-elections being fought in Surbiton — two seats on the local council, the third for a seat on the GLC.

BRITANNIC HOUSE

The privileged pupils of
one of the country's most
exclusive schools, Harrow,
file out of their classes.

LET'S GET PHYSICAL

Above: Social worker Roger Rolfe (in blue track suit) supervises a five-a-side football match between handicapped players in the Sobell Centre. The weekly matches, which alternate with netball, have led to remarkable improvements in physical co-ordination amongst the players. Many participants who previously could barely walk are now adept at both sports.

Right: Polaroids of rehearsals for 'Swan Lake' at The Royal Ballet.

Following page, left: A Sikh waits for free legal advice from volunteers at the Southall Rights Community Centre. A thousand citizens of Southall, which houses the largest Asian community in London, use the Centre each year to solve their legal problems.

Following page, right: Sales assistant Raymond Hatchings attends to a customer in the legal outfitters Ede and Ravenscroft of Chancery Lane. The company has been supplying wigs, robes and ceremonial splendour to kings, dukes and judges since 1689.

CHRISTOPHER CORMACK

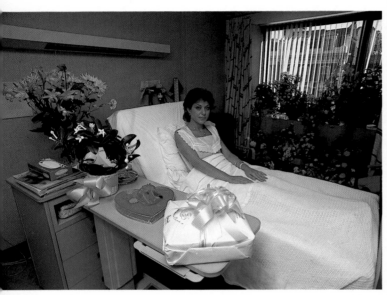

| THE NATIONAL HEALTH | 11.30 AM |

Mrs Fadlallah from the Lebanon (above) recuperates in the Cromwell Hospital in Earls Court, a private hospital which is the medical equivalent of a five star hotel. Medically one of the most advanced hospitals in Europe, the Cromwell also offers its patients luxurious post-operative accommodation, including colour television and in-house video movies, a secretarial staff and telex facilities for businessmen, and a cordon bleu cuisine more suited to a cruise liner than a hospital. Meanwhile, across the city in Plumstead, Mrs Madden (right), bedridden in her flat, receives her only meal of the day from Meals on Wheels — sausages and mash, courtesy of the National Health Service.

Previous page: Family Reunion — The Vora family on the balcony of their flat in Cranleigh Gardens, Southall. It is a double celebration for Abeda Vora (right) and her five-month-old son. Not only has grandmother Isabein (centre) been allowed entry to visit her grandson, but the Voras have recently been moved from the dreaded Golf Links Estate, where racial violence runs high, to the more pleasant surroundings of Cranleigh Gardens.

STUART FRANKLIN

JANE BOWN

HEAD OVER HEELS

Morning break at St Peter's Primary School, Eaton Square. The children are playing one of their favourite games.

Left: Bousfield Junior Mixed and Infants School (from left) Monica Meira, Kathleen Cruz, Shanaz Khan, Hansatu Ado.

Previous page, left: Jimmy, a long-time 'character' in Leather Lane market.

Previous page, right: The craftsmen, staff and bells of the Whitechapel Bell Foundry, makers of the Liberty Bell, Bow Bells, the bells of Westminster, and the most famous bell of all, Big Ben. The foundry first began casting bells in 1420 in Aldgate; a century later it moved to its present site in Whitechapel. Today it is one of only two survivors from an industry which, during the 17th century, numbered more than thirty bell foundries within the city boundaries alone. "I hope we'll survive" says director Mr W.A. Hughes. "My son is carrying on. We are currently casting two peals of bells for the U.S.A. — one for Miami Cathedral, the other for a college chapel in Kalamazoo."

SUBURBIA

Above: The hedge at 29 Ash Grove, South Ealing, belongs to 69-year-old Mr Kiel, a retired precision engineer. Although not a topiarist, he started clipping it into shape in 1977 'because the road sign was missing'. It took two years to reach its present form; now all it requires is a trim every three weeks during the growing season. Mr Kiel's hedge really came into its own during the Silver Jubilee, however, sprouting crowns, shields and other royal motifs.

Right: A Sikh coping with the English elements in Ealing.

SCHOOL'S OUT

Lunch break for the 106 pupils of Harbinger Primary School on the Isle of Dogs. The walls of the 100-year-old building are decorated with murals painted by a local community group; this one is of the *Harbinger*, a clipper ship from the same era as the *Cutty Sark* which lies permanently moored at Greenwich, a stone's throw across the river. "It's an old school, but it's friendly," says headmistress Vikki Segbeer. "It has character." Her pupils, a small United Nations of ethnic minorities — Asian, West Indian, Vietnamese — are inclined to agree.

THE NAKED LUNCH   12.30 PM

Debbie makes up in her dressing room, a tiny, bare room in the Golden Lion pub in Fulham, before her lunchtime striptease engagement in the adjoining bar. Debbie does not consider herself a professional stripper. A housewife with children, she strips simply to 'make ends meet'. Her act bears little relationship to the exotica of Soho and the West End.

loody

DON McCULLIN

CLOCKING ON   1.10 PM

The clientele of the Clock
Pub in Leather Lane, many
of them stall holders in
Leather Lane market,
enjoy a lunchtime pint,
or two.

Previous page: Brick Lane,
Whitechapel. Throughout
the week Brick Lane is a
warren of poverty, racism
and neglect. It is only on
Sunday mornings when the
Lane and its surrounding
streets are choked with
street vendors, barrows
and bargain hunters,
that Cockney life returns
to the East End.

JOHN LONDEI

PILLARS OF POWER

Michael Jenkins (left) and
John Barkshire, Chief
Executive and Chairman
of the Board of the London
International Finance
Futures Exchange, on
the steps of their 'office',
the Royal Exchange, next
to the Bank of England.
The Futures Exchange
provides the opportunity
for businesses subject
to fluctuations in currency
and interest rates to
offload the risk. Opened
in September 1982, the
Futures Exchange is the
City's newest money
market. So far it has made
what Michael Jenkins
modestly calls 'a good
start'. ''Today, for example,
our turnover was £1½
billion. And that was quite
a low day.''

RICK CORDELL

NATURE LOVERS

Far right: Street cleaner John McKibben shelters from the rain in Charlotte Street.

Above: Walter Hall and Regina Jansen, both aged 20, in Hyde Park.

Right: Charles, a retired railway worker, cycles to Wimbledon Common each day 'for a bit of peace and quiet'.

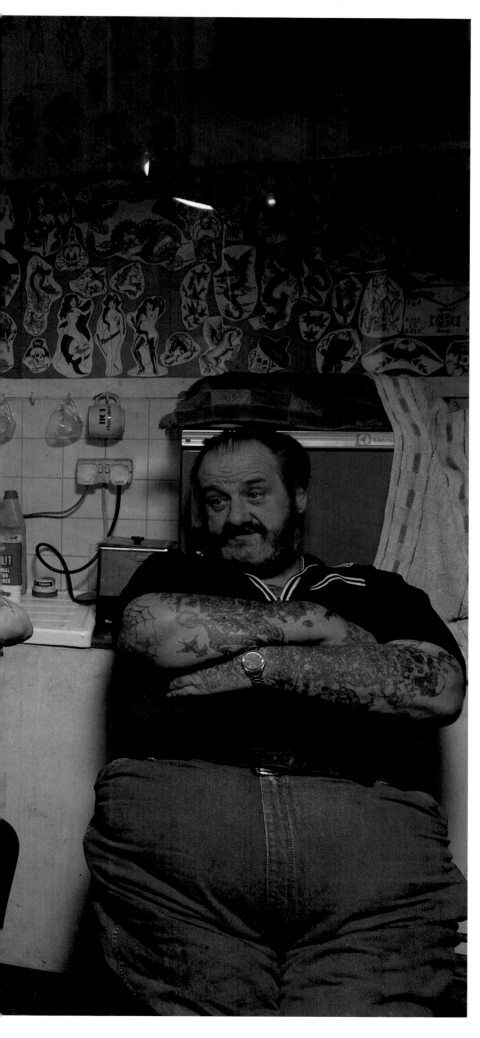

Ted tattoos John, a regular at Jock's Tattooing Studio in the Pentonville Road. John has more than 50 tattoos on his body. Jock, sitting opposite, after 40 years in the business, has collected 800. Although he claims to have adorned the skins of many of the famous, Jock divulges no names. "Just make sure the punters know they've got to be 18 before I'll come near them with a needle."

Following page: Madame Tussaud's, a tourist Mecca, housing perhaps the world's most disconcertingly life-like collection of waxworks. A recent innovation has been to remove the rope barriers separating the exhibits from the spectators, allowing customers to pose with the famous or infamous. Here a real infant sits with a wax Chelsea Pensioner, and a group of real Saudi children pose beside the wax former King of Saudi Arabia, H.M. Malik, Faisal bin Abdul Aziz al Saud.

129

GUARDIANS AT THE GATES OF KNOWLEDGE

A gatekeeper of the Natural History Museum waits anxiously for the afternoon's onslaught of school children.

Right: Gatekeepers at the British Museum, repository of such treasures as the Elgin Marbles, the Rosetta Stone, the largest collection of mummified Pharoahs outside Egypt and the 10 million volumes of the British Library Reading Room, where the young Karl Marx wrote capitalism's obituary, 'Das Kapital'.

Previous page: Lunch break for chic shoppers in South Molton Street.

Following page: A lone angler braving the rain on Hampstead Heath.

PENTONVILLE

A guard looking for escape equipment or weapons conducts a spot search in Pentonville.

Top right: A 'cleaner' scrubs the floor of a prison corridor. All prisoners in Pentonville are assigned jobs, and all work within the prison is done by the prisoners themselves.

Bottom right: Prisoners' 'period of association', two hours every week — or every two weeks, depending on the number of prison officers available — when inmates are allowed to mix with their fellow prisoners. Most, however, elect simply to watch television.

Previous page: Governor's Adjudication: A prisoner charged with breaking prison rules toes the line before the Governor in Pentonville Prison.

MIKE ABRAHAMS

DOING TIME

An inmate during prisoners' 'period of association', free to lounge on the landing outside his cell.

Left: Prior to 'association period'.

Following page: Visiting day at Pentonville Prison — half an hour only.

MIKE ABRAHAMS

141

144

SALLY FEAR

A SINGLE AND TWO DOUBLES   1.30 PM

Onie and Alan Hardcastle are married at the Chelsea Registry Office.

Left: A lone drinker at the Smithfield Tavern.

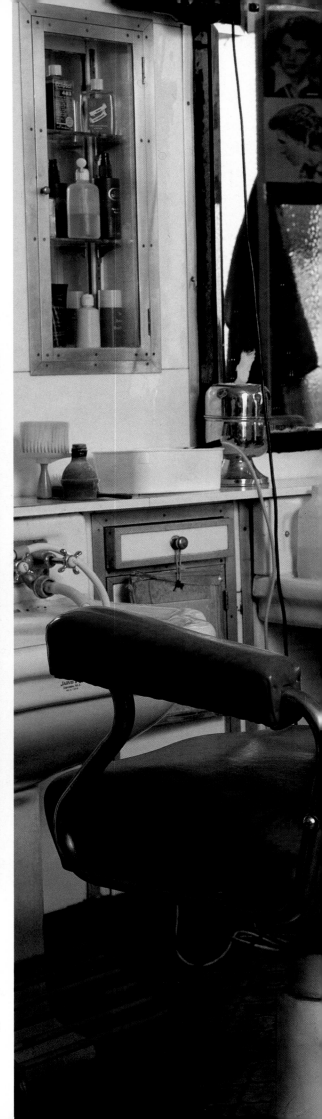

CLIP JOINTS

Right: Savvas Theodossi relaxes in his shop on the Fulham Broadway in the midst of a busy day snipping short backs and sides. The shop dates back to the turn of the century, long before the days of male perms and blow waves. Although Savvas, originally from Cyprus, has been in Britain for a considerably shorter period of time — some 35 years — he too prefers the traditional approach to hairdressing, as befits a man who served his apprenticeship in the barber's shop which groomed the late Archbishop Makarios.

Above: Hip hairdresser in Kensington Market. Ken Market is the home of the most avant garde of London's outlandish street fashions and hair is cut to match.

MARKET DAY   1.50 PM

Stall holders on Camden Market look resigned to rather miserable mid-week takings. A maze of shops, barrows and stalls, the market, situated behind a lock on the Regent's Canal, has overtaken Portobello Road as trendy London's favourite scavenging ground.

Previous page: Staff and patrons respond to the photocall outside an East End cafe.

Punk guitarist, Hackney.

Following page: Dealers in gilt-edged government securities, resplendent in *de rigueur* top hats, conspire in the corridors leading to the floor of the Stock Exchange.

MOTOR CITY

A shift at the Ford plant in Dagenham swings into gear. Nine thousand men work on the Dagenham production lines in the assembly and body shops (shown here), 40% of them on the night shift. It takes four days to build a car from scratch; 850 finished automobiles roll off the production line each day.

Previous page: Louisa Stanislas operates one of the last manual packing lines at the highly automated McVittie's biscuit factory in Harlesdon.

Following pages: Youths in Brick Lane.

STUART FRANKLIN

BEDS AND REDS   2.15 PM

Hospital workers demonstrate against the closure of a children's ward, outside the Paddington Area Health Authority office in New Wharf Road.

Right: Ken Livingstone, left wing leader of the Labour-controlled Greater London Council, the governing body of London, stands beside the Peace Year banner at County Hall. During his stormy term of office, 'Red Ken's' actions, such as halving transport fares, inviting members of Sinn Fein to London, and declaring the capital a Nuclear Free Zone have infuriated his Tory opponents in the Government to such an extent that they have introduced legislation to scrap the GLC altogether.

Previous page: The Mothball Fleet: A ship rusts silently beside the deserted Victoria Docks, Canning Town.

Following page: London Transport bus conductor Vivian Bell takes her scheduled break at Chalk Farm Garage during her shift on the Number 3 bus route. Vivian's shift takes her from Chalk Farm to Crystal Palace .

eace Year 1983

GLC

Working for London and P

JOBS FOR A CHANGE

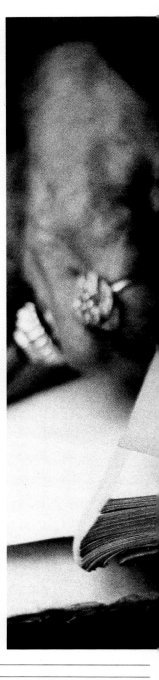

PIPE DREAMS

Right: Dennis Callwood never stopped using his Leica — even when he had an afternoon cup of tea in an Oxford Street cafe.

Left: Waiting patiently for the ferry at Westminster Pier.

BUSINESS AND PLEASURE   2.30 PM

Left: Outside, 'The Old Lady of Threadneedle Street', the Bank of England. Meanwhile (above), no less of an institution is in full swing — tea at The Ritz.

BACK TO FRONT

Above: Mayfair.

Right: 58-year-old George Nosworthy has been greeting guests for 15 years in his job as link man for The Ritz. "The job dates from the time of horses and carriages when the link man used to take the links — or traces — off the horses. He also used to keep the front clear of what the horses left behind." Now the link man's job is to welcome visitors, see their luggage safely inside, and provide them with directions about town. "I enjoy it. I like meeting people and it's a good variety of work."

Following page: Members of the capital's growing army of unemployed scan the jobs on offer at the Government Job Centre in Battersea. With London's unemployed standing at 370,885, the prospects of an individual's finding something suitable are slim.

TIPS ON
B HUNTING
FINDING
HE RIGHT
JOB
AKE A LEAFLET NOW!
FINDING
THE RIGHT
JOB
TIPS ON
IS ILL HEALTH,
INJURY, OR
DISABILITY,
MAKING IT DIFFICULT
TO FIND OR KEEP
A JOB? 1st FLOOR
TOPS

CATCH A

TRAINING

SCHEDULE

HERE

sk about free

training with pay.

Just kicking
around?

See what your
JOBCENTRE
can do for
you!

CAR PARK

We'll look
the pen
while y
after
poun

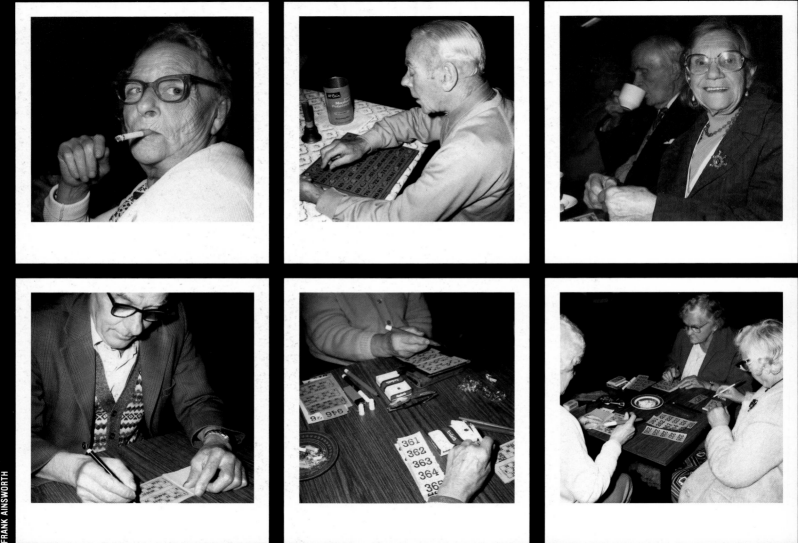

ANITA CORBIN

EYES DOWN

Regulars at the Mecca Empire Bingo Hall in Mare Street, Hackney, concentrate on the call. Once celebrated as the most famous music hall in the East End, the Empire long ago fell victim to Londoners' unshakeable passion for bingo. Four thousand players pass through its portals each week — a third of them pensioners — each determined to win the top prize of £50. With the possibility of losing up to £10 a session, any slight interruption to a player's concentration causes tempers to become rapidly frayed, as photographer Anita Corbin soon discovered.

Left: A highlight in the week of the residents of the Sir Oswald Stoll Mansion Estate in Fulham is their bingo game. They pay 25p per card to play and the prizes are mostly non perishable such as tinned foods, tea etc. with occasionally a £1 or £1.50 cash prize. Another attraction is the free tea and biscuits. All are a welcome supplement to a meagre pension.

LEON MORRIS

ANDREW CROWLEY

STREET SURVIVORS   2.45 PM

Above: A 'shopping bag lady', well known around Soho, pushes her worldly possessions before her up Wardour Street.

Left: Father and son street traders — 'No names, please' — in Camden Passage.

Top: The indignities at Paddington Green Police Station.

BRICKS AND MORTAR

Construction workers,
Bethnall Green Road.

181

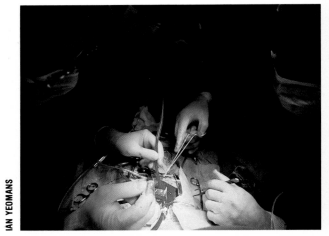

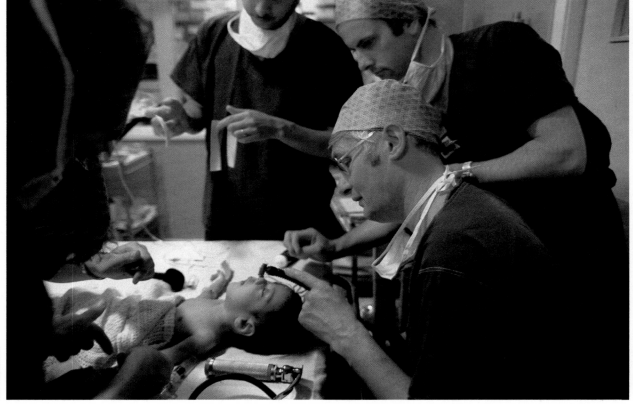

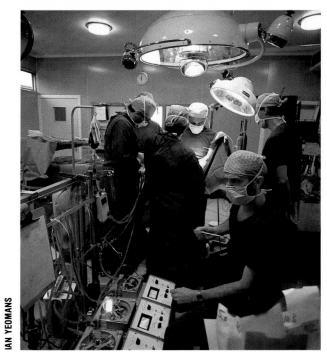

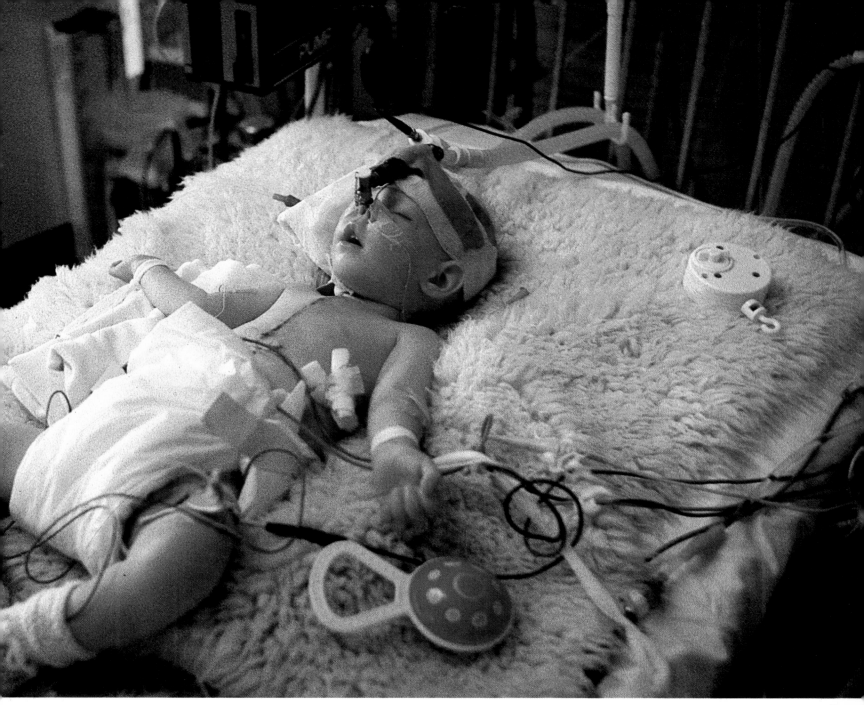

OPEN HEART SURGERIES

Left: Doctors at Harefield Hospital's Pediatric Surgical Unit (centre) anaesthetise 4-month-old Daniel Ferns prior to performing open heart surgery. Daniel is suffering from a condition known as 'total anomalous posterior pulmonary venous drainage'. Without the operation his life expectancy is negligible.

Bottom: The team of surgeons, led by Egyptian-born Magdi Yacoub, begins the high technology assault to correct Daniel's anomaly.

Top: Working on Daniel's exposed heart.

Above: Fifteen-month-old Laura Barnfather recuperates in Harefield's Intensive Treatment Unit following an operation to correct a transposition of the great arteries (known as 'the switch'). Like Daniel, Laura's life expectancy would have been greatly diminished without the operation. Like Daniel's, her operation is a complete success.

ERICA LENNARD

FOREIGN CLIME

A visitor from the Middle East strolls through unaccustomed drizzle near the Serpentine in Hyde Park.

Eight children ranging in ages from six years to fourteen years were supplied with autofocus Canon Sureshots for the day.These three pages are representative of the quality work they supplied.

HIGHBURY SCHOOL   ROISON GALVIN AGED 8

OFF TO SCHOOL   EVE LIGHT AGED 7

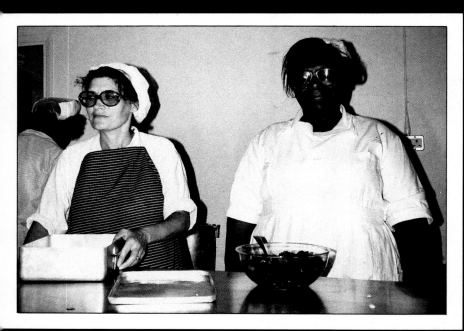

DINNER LADIES, ST MARY MAGDALEN SCHOOL   LEAH CAMPBELL AGED 6

BBC CAMERA CREW   EMMA KNIGHT AGED 9

DEBORAH AND TANYA GOLDSOBEL AGED 12 AND 14

PLAYMATES HENNA FLOSSIE AND CHRISTABEL  LEAH CAMPBELL AGED 6

HIGHBURY SCHOOL   LIAM GALVIN AGED 10   TERRY LEFTIN   AGED 8   SELF PORTRAIT   JESSICA HUDDLE AGED 6

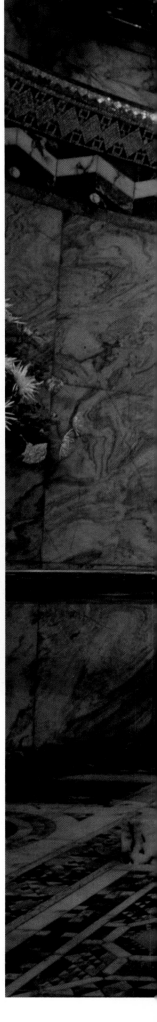

JEREMY NICHOLL

"ON YOUR KNEES!"

At Quex Road, Kilburn, mass is held in the Church of the Sacred Heart, the main Catholic church in the area. Although Kilburn is a predominantly Irish area and the local priests tend to be Irish too, on this occasion the mass is taken by Father Corsini Perera from Sri Lanka.

Right: St Bartholomew's The Less, the Parish church at Barts Hospital. Originally part of a Priory built in 1123, it was partly razed by Henry VIII in 1526 before being rebuilt in 1789. Today it is used by the patients and staff of the hospital for services, christenings, weddings, but never funerals. A burial pit during the Black Death in 1342 and again during the plague of 1660, the ground surrounding it is now filled with bones. 'It's the reason our plane trees do so well,' says the Vicar, Rev. R.H. Arnold. 'All that calcium . . . !'

Previous page: Omar and Dara from Nigeria strolling through Kensington Gardens.

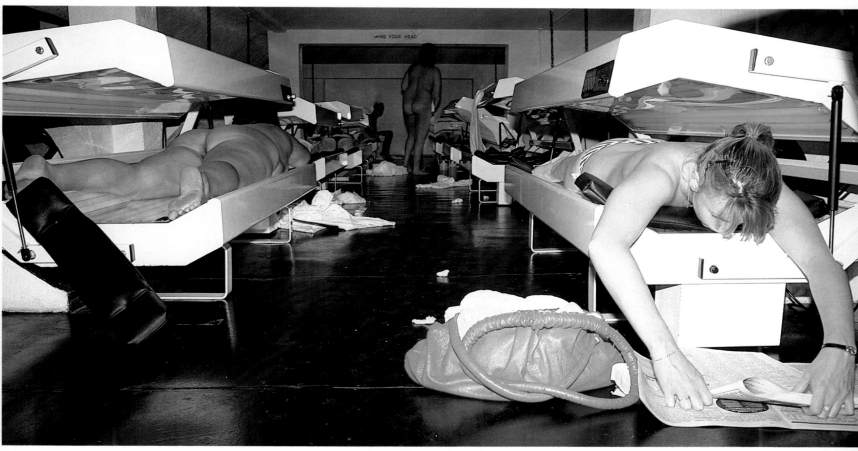

TROPICAL LONDON 3.15 PM

Sybaritic customers soak up the steamy pleasures of The Sanctuary, a slice of the tropics the size of a small office block in Covent Garden. Complete with tropical birds overhead and exotic fish underwater, The Sanctuary offers London's well-heeled females fitness and lazy luxury in the form of a pool (left), sun room (above), saunas, jacuzzis and a range of beauty treatments.

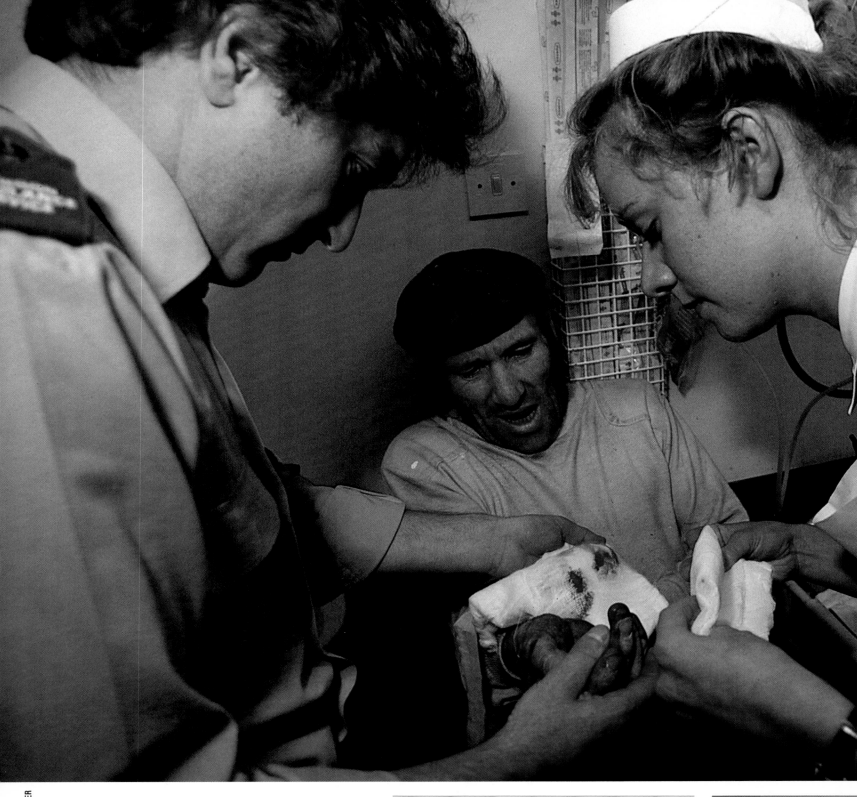

MIKE GOLDWATER

BOWLED OVER

Above and right: National Health Service patients in the casualty wards at London Hospital, Whitechapel.

Top right: Ambulancemen administer first aid to a traffic accident victim knocked down on Waterloo Bridge. More than 14,000 pedestrians are injured by motorists each year in the metropolitan area. The ambulance service, for its part, attends 2,000 emergency calls every day, ranging from heart attacks to premature births.

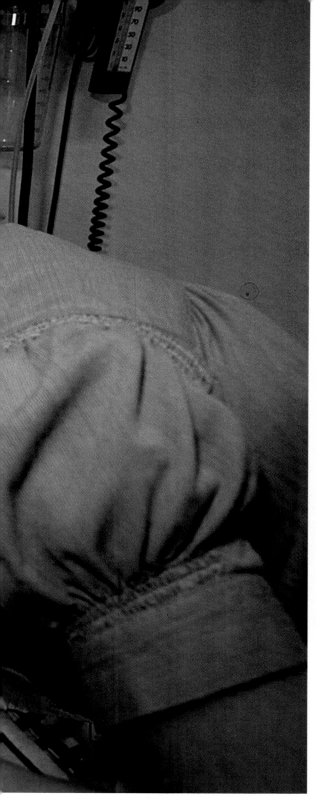

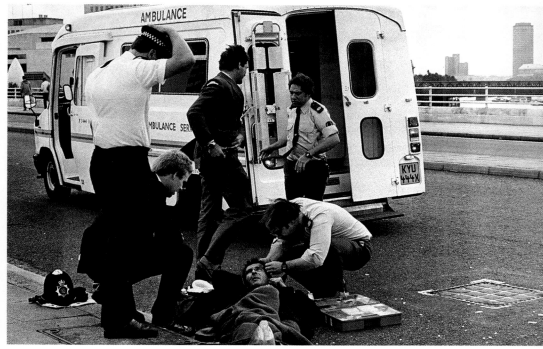

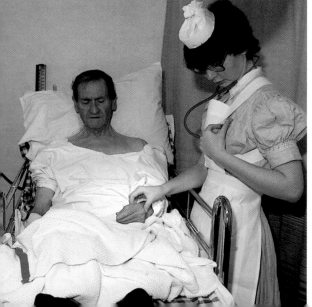

WILLIAM KLEIN

ON THE BALL

Rugby practice at Harrow School on the first day of term after the holidays.

Left: Body builders pumping iron in the Sobell Sports Centre, Holloway. Three-quarters of a million Londoners use the council-run centre each year. Its facilities range from ice skating to the martial arts, but fitness training remains the most popular pastime.

Following page: George Callard, who has been caring for London Zoo's orang-utans for 47 years, with some of his charges — Suka and her baby, Jago. A third orang-utan is kept in the same enclosure as Suka and her baby to learn how to be a mother when it is time for her to be mated.

SCRAP YARD BOW

Sandwiched between motorways, seven storeys of grim council flats and the match factory of the famous nineteenth-century match girls' strike, lies this graveyard of the XJ6's. The residents of the flats spend their daylight hours with the constant racket of the great crunching machines mangling once carefully polished motors into neat bale-sized bricks.

Previous page: Canal bridge, Camden Town.

DEREK RIDGERS

THE HARD SELL

Fashion designer Jane Kahn in her bedroom, in a semi-derelict house in Holloway. Her clothes, which she sells from her shop Kahniverous in King's Road's Great Gear Market, create shockwaves even on Chelsea's fashionably futuristic streets.

Right: The stars of the Queensway furniture store's 'Big Q' sale. Through saturation radio and television advertising, Queensway has elevated the once-a-year sale to a permanent condition. At Queensway, every day is sale day.

205

NUMBER PLEASE

Above: Police cadets at the Hendon Police Training Centre are instructed in the art of booking offending motorists.

Top right: The long wait for a policeman to come and unclamp her car proves too much for one illegally — and expensively — parked motorist in Hanover Square.

Right: Stoke Newington.

THE WRITINGS ON THE WALL

An exercise walk in the West End.

Right: Bus queue outside Kings Cross station.

Far right: IRA graffiti, Kilburn Square.

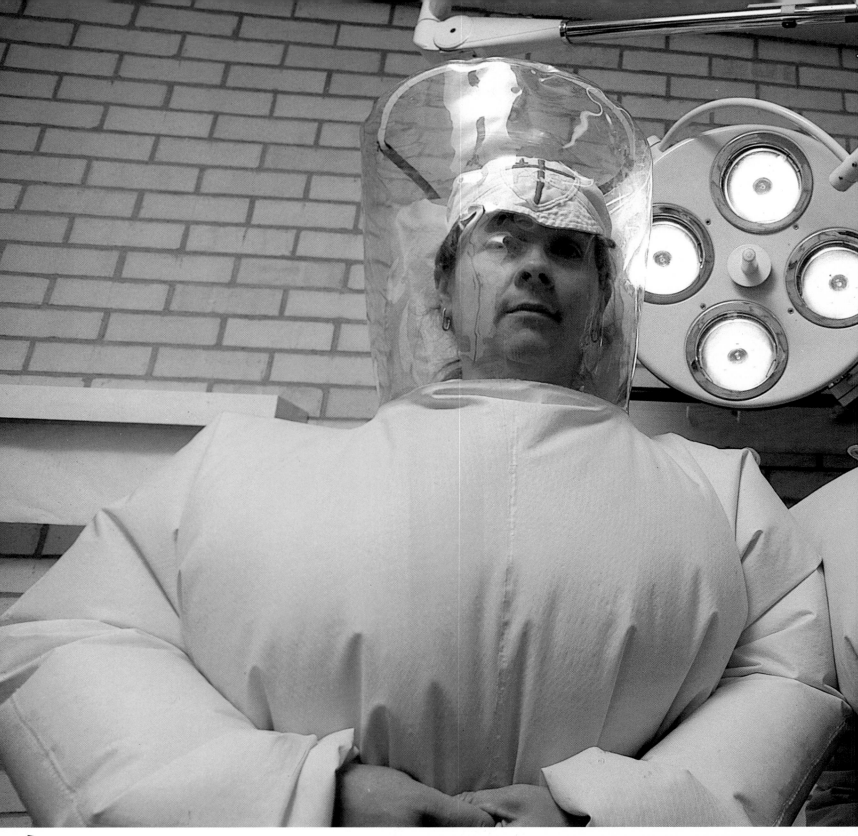

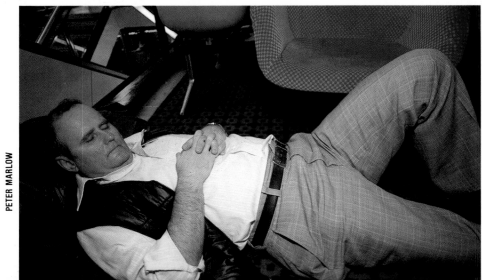

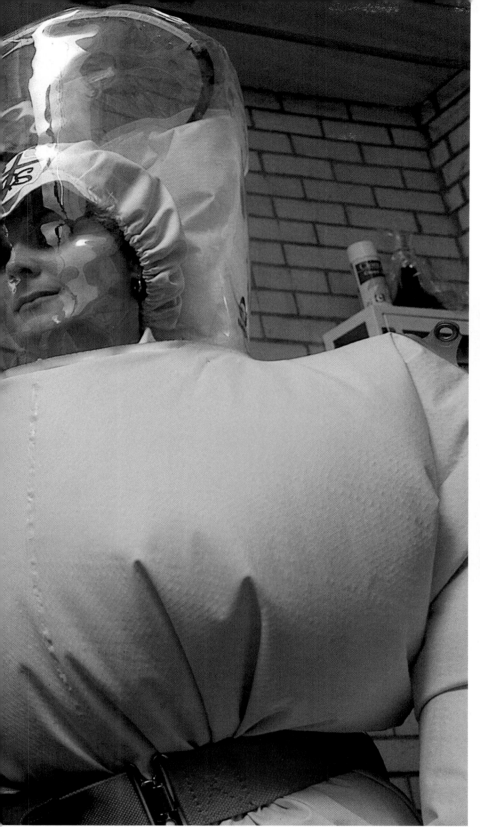

DRESSED FOR THE OCCASION

Top left: Linda Peacock and Elizabeth Knowles dressed for work in the Quarantine Centre at Heathrow Airport. The respirator suits protect against air-transmitted diseases such as rabies.

Above: A small — and very frightened — transit passenger waits for his flight to be announced. All animals, even those in transit, are kept in the Quarantine Centre.

Left: Passengers resting on the way home to Europe.

Following page: Sixty-one-year-old George McDowell, suffering from pneumonia, receives a visit from his National Health GP in his council flat overlooking the Roman Road market. The area, with its high percentage of poor, solitary and elderly, has the highest incidence of illness in the United Kingdom — everything from VD to TB — a situation with which the already over-stretched National Health Service has difficulty in coping. New government plans to cut services further will mean that the area's health levels will continue to deteriorate.

SALLY FEAR

GLAD RAGS   3.30 PM

Claire, Bean and Hazel, assistants at the King's Road clothing store Boy, with a local from Chelsea. Boy was one of the first — and most famous — punk shops in London.

Right: Ada Moss of Plumstead, south east London, celebrates her 97th birthday with a lunch from Meals on Wheels and a birthday cake which she shares with her life-long friend Lillian, aged 98. It is an emotional reunion: the two have not seen each other for six years.

HIGH LIFE

Joseph Cassar surveys the bleakness of derelict dock lands from the balcony of his flat in Rotherhithe. His is one of the few flats in the area without a sheet of plywood nailed over the front door. When he first moved in seven years ago he was surrounded by neighbours. Now, with the decline of the docks, less than a handful remain. Joseph is waiting desperately to be rehoused.

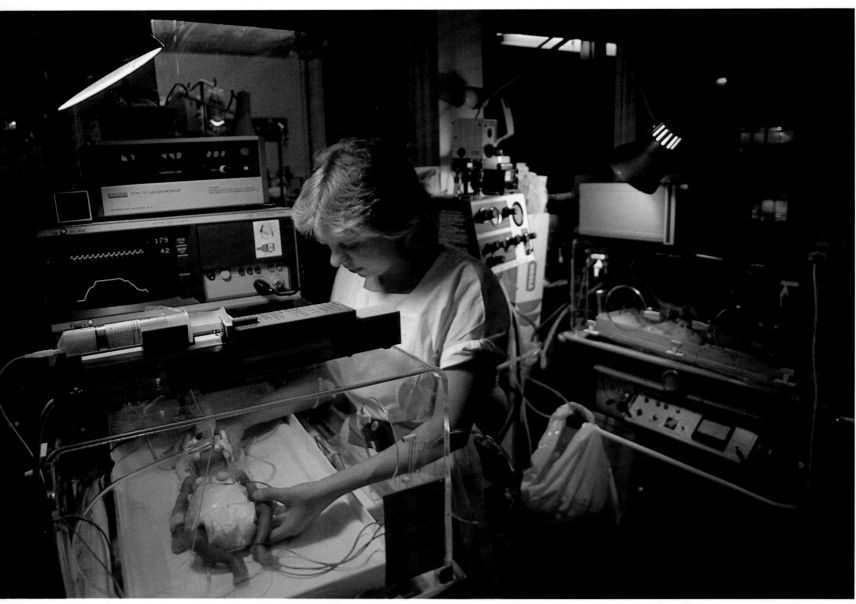

NEW LONDONERS

Above: Premature baby unit at the London Hospital, Whitechapel.

Right: Less than 20 minutes after his birth, Janette Brocking breastfeeds her new son, Adam Keith, for the first time. He was born in the South London Hospital for Women in Clapham, a unique establishment. Not only is it the only hospital in London where women are treated by other women, but it also offers facilities for mothers to give birth in whatever position they feel most comfortable. Janette gave birth to Adam — her second child — lying on a soft mat on the hospital floor, an event witnessed by her husband Keith.

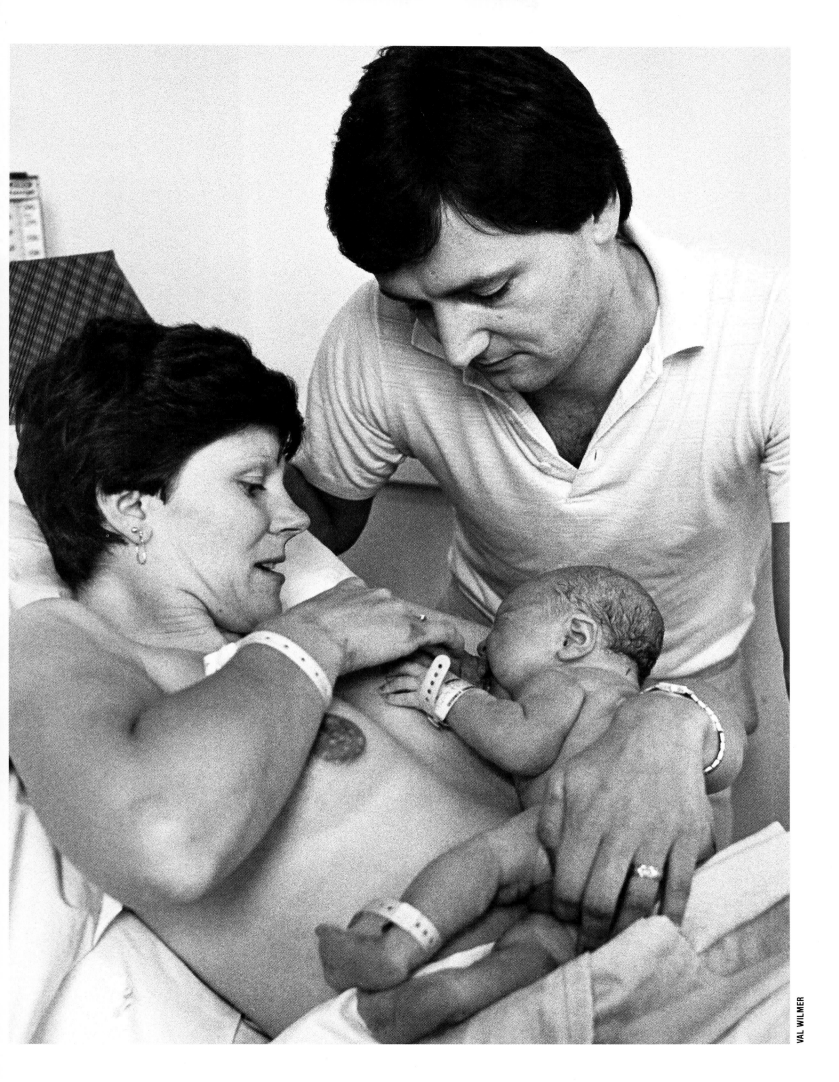

SUE PACKER

UNIFORM APPROACH

Master Nicholas Johnson, 7, returns home to Parsons Green after a day at his private Belgravia prep school, Eaton House. Nicholas has attended Eaton House for two years and likes it very much. "So he ought to. It's bloody well expensive enough!" says his father. At £425 a term he has a point.

Right: A member of the Horse Guards directs his colleagues through the traffic down The Mall.

221

HOT SPOT 4.0 PM

Porchester Hall Turkish Baths, Queensway. Twenty-eight thousand men and women gently poach themselves in the steamy bowels of Porchester Hall every year. Built in 1929, it offers showers, hot rooms, a steam room and an icy plunge pool set in surroundings resembling something from ancient Rome. For £6.60 customers can remain there for as long as they wish — all day, if they want to risk turning into prunes. And afterwards there's a cup of tea and a plate of scrambled eggs on toast in your own private cubicle!

ARMET FRANCIS

THE PORTABLE STUDIO

Right: Photographer Armet Francis realised early on in the day that as he couldn't find suitable subjects, they would have to come to him. So he took his director's chair, set up his own sidewalk 'studio' beside a cracked wall in Royal Crescent, West London, and invited passers-by to pose for his camera. "Most of them thought I was mad!" Those who didn't included three West Indian youths (top left) who took great delight in ridiculing the whole proceedings until dared to pose by a friend of Armet ; a Portuguese woman (top right) out shopping — "I have a camera, I take pictures too"; an unruffled Indian businessman (bottom left); and an entire local football team.

Above: Three women out on the town in Kensington.

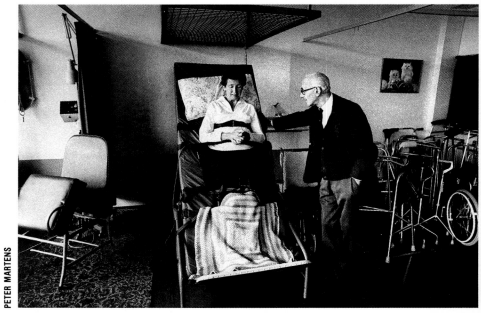

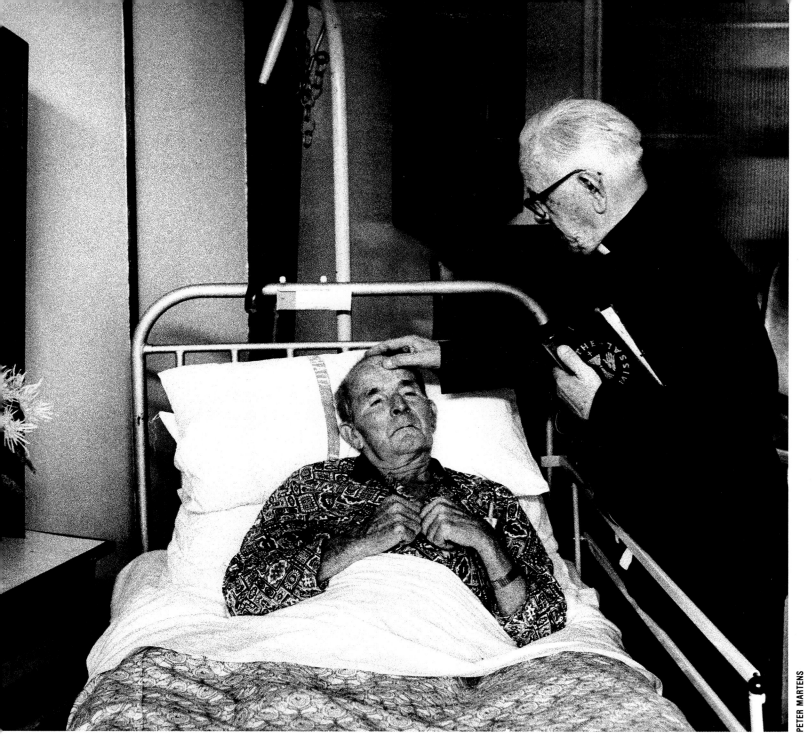

LAST REFUGE

St Joseph's Hospice in Mare Street, Hackney, has been providing comfort and care to terminally ill East Enders since its first patient — a 47-year-old Hackney train driver dying of consumption — was carried through its doors by his friends on January 14, 1900. Founded by the Irish Sisters of Charity to provide a last refuge for the poor of the London slums, St Joseph's now has 112 beds and has established itself as a pioneer of pain control and terminal care.

HARRY BENSON

THE OTHER HALF

Above: Gerald Cavendish Grosvenor, 15th Baronet of Eton, 9th Baron Grosvenor, 9th Viscount Belgrave, 9th Earl Grosvenor, 8th Marquis of Westminster, 6th Duke of Westminster which last title is the one by which he is commonly known.

On his birthday his brother-in-law, photographer Lord Litchfield, presented him with a Monopoly board marked with the properties he rents out in real life.

Although reputedly Britain's richest man with assets in excess of 1000 million pounds including 150 of London's most select and expensive hectares, a great part of his time is spent as chairman, patron, or in membership of fund-raising organisations for the deprived and disabled.

Right: Council house tenant, Notting Hill Gate.

AKIRA KOBAYASHI

DECAYING DOCKLANDS   5.0 PM

Bermondsey is an area which died with the closure of the Thames docks. Now the largest piece of vacant real estate in the centre of any European city, the Docklands have been earmarked as the development area of the 1980s, a potential bonanza which has set property developers and speculators against local councils such as Bermondsey. Whatever the outcome, one thing remains certain. Communities like Bermondsey, their residents long gone, will never be as they were, a fact underlined by the picture bottom right. Today, all that remains of Bermondsey's Downtown Tenants' Association is the sign.

Left: Battersea Bridge.

HOMEWARD BOUND

The rush back to
the suburbs across
London Bridge.

WILLIAM KLEIN

THE PICK OF THE CROP 5.30 PM

Scavenging for leftovers, Brick Lane.

235

TIM MERCER

GORGEOUS GEORGE AND THE MAD HATTER

Hat designer extraordinaire David Shilling, famed for the outrageous millinery he created for his mother for Ascot each year. David has slipped into something more comfortable for the evening — a bright pink lame jacket and a gold shirt, set off by a small Venetian mask.

Left: George Melly, jazz singer, author, broadcaster and a celebrated member of Soho low-life, relaxes in his bedroom with a glass of champagne after yet another photo session.

Members of the Monday Club, the Conservative Party's influential right wing 'ginger group', gather before the evening's meeting.

WILLIAM KLEIN

LIMBS AND LAUGHTER

Music business 'face' Magenta and fashion designer Martin Degville need little incentive to pose in one of the Camden Palace nightclub's many corridors.

Right: Barbara Bellingham took women's legs as her assignment. For the day she reported complete co-operation and a great deal of mirth. So involved did she become that she forgot her parked car — but the police didn't. They towed it away!

SMOKE FILLED ROOMS

Mayfair clubland: Burberry coats on marble walls.

Right: Gentleman's Club, St James.

243

BARRY LEWIS

THE QUICK AND THE DEAD

Above: A scrapyard by Barking Creek, the end of the road for a luxury Austin Princess.

Right: Jack Barclay's Rolls-Royce showroom in Berkeley Square, Mayfair. 'It was quite extraordinary,' recalls Dutch photographer Aart Aan de Wiel. 'Even though it was dark, there were a couple of people polishing the cars.'

245

GUGLIELMO GALVIN

SETTING THE SCENE

Top, left: A worried David Hockney undertakes a hurried final inspection of his backdrops for Ravel's *L'Enfant et les Sortileges* at the Royal Opera House.

Above: Irish artist Sean Hillen in his studio close to London Bridge. His works are unique religious icons; one of his most recent is a computerised Christ which talks.

Left: Scenery painter Graham Barkley in front of his latest work, an exotic oriental location commissioned by Leeds Television.

ERIC WATSON

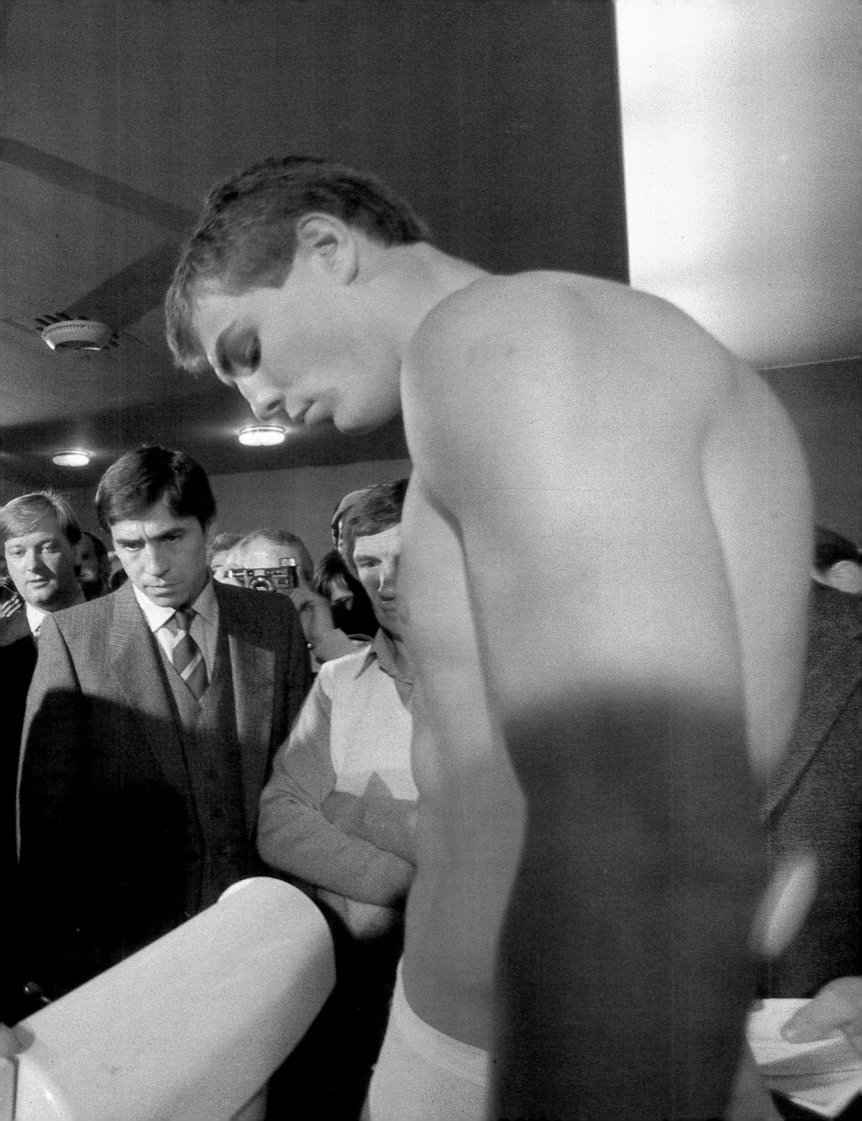

BARRY LEWIS

THE FIGHT GAME

Wednesday was fight night at London's Alexandra Palace. It was also the night contender Mark Kaylor knocked out British middleweight champ Roy Gumms in the fifth round. Kaylor was carried shoulder high around the ring after the bout by his overjoyed fans and spent most of the rest of the evening posing for photographers with his handlers and his manager, Terry Lawless (bottom left). The preliminary bout between Anders Ekland and Paddy Finn ended with Finn on hands and knees on the canvas (bottom right). Above: World flyweight champion Charlie Magri after working out in the gym above the Royal Oak Pub in Barking, East London. Top left: The punters.

Previous page: At the Bloomsbury Crest Hotel, Russell Square, middleweight contender Mark Kaylor tips the scales for Britain's boxing press before his title fight against champion Roy Gumms. Later, Gumms is on his back, and Kaylor is the new British Middleweight Champion.

WHERE THERE'S SMOKE . . .

Above: Mr Croley, managing director of cigar merchants Robert Lewis of St James, checks his customers' reserved stocks. Cigars are expensive at Robert Lewis's. The boxes to Mr Croley's right, all reserved by one man, are worth £49,500. What else would be expected from the store which supplied Sir Winston Churchill with the finest Havanas?

Right: The famous Oscar of the Waldorf, manager of the Waldorf Restaurant, Palm Court and Club Bar, flambés one of his celebrated crêpes. Holder of the International Trophy and Gold Medal for crepe Suzettes and cocktails, Oscar is also a fellow of the elite International Academy of Flambiers, an honour bestowed only on seven others worldwide.

253

HOMER SYKES

ROUND THE CLOCK SERVICE

Right: The drivers of Transport Unlimited, an all-Irish mini-cab company on the Holloway Road which serves the large community in North London. Transport Unlimited survives in a fiercely competitive business by accepting any job, no matter how small, at any time of the day or night. The drivers are just beginning to hit their stride; half an hour later they are all out on the road and the office is deserted.

Above: The mini-cab's keenest competitor, the traditional 'black' cab.

Following page, left: Wet York stones of the Westminster Embankment.

Following page, right: The Last Lamp Lighter: Mr Bullard on his rounds lighting the way for the law clerks, barristers and judges of the Middle Temple. An employee of North Thames Gas, Mr Bullard is a gaslamp lighter — the last lamp lighter in London. His hours are totally flexible, ranging from three in the afternoon to late in the evening, depending upon when the sun sets. He likes his job even though, as he admits, it is a very solitary trade.

GUGLIELMO GALVIN

257

LONG TERM PROSPECT

Bernard Moragrega Ferras counts the evening's takings upstairs in the a la carte restaurant at the *Prospect Of Whitby*, London's oldest riverside inn. The *Prospect* has occupied the same site on Wapping Wall since 1520. Now it is the fashionable haunt of celebrities, catering to such titled diners as Princess Margaret.

Right: Robin Leigh-Pemberton, Governor of the Bank of England, with the ledger recording the bank's first day of trading on July 27, 1694. Founded in the reign of William III, the bank was originally part of the Grocers' Hall in Princess Street. In 1734 it was moved to its current site in Threadneedle Street, thereby earning its affectionate city name The Old Lady Of Threadneedle Street.

Following page, left: Father Roberto Russo in St Peter's Church, Clerkenwell.

Following page, right: Style mongers at Camden Palace and The Batcave.

259

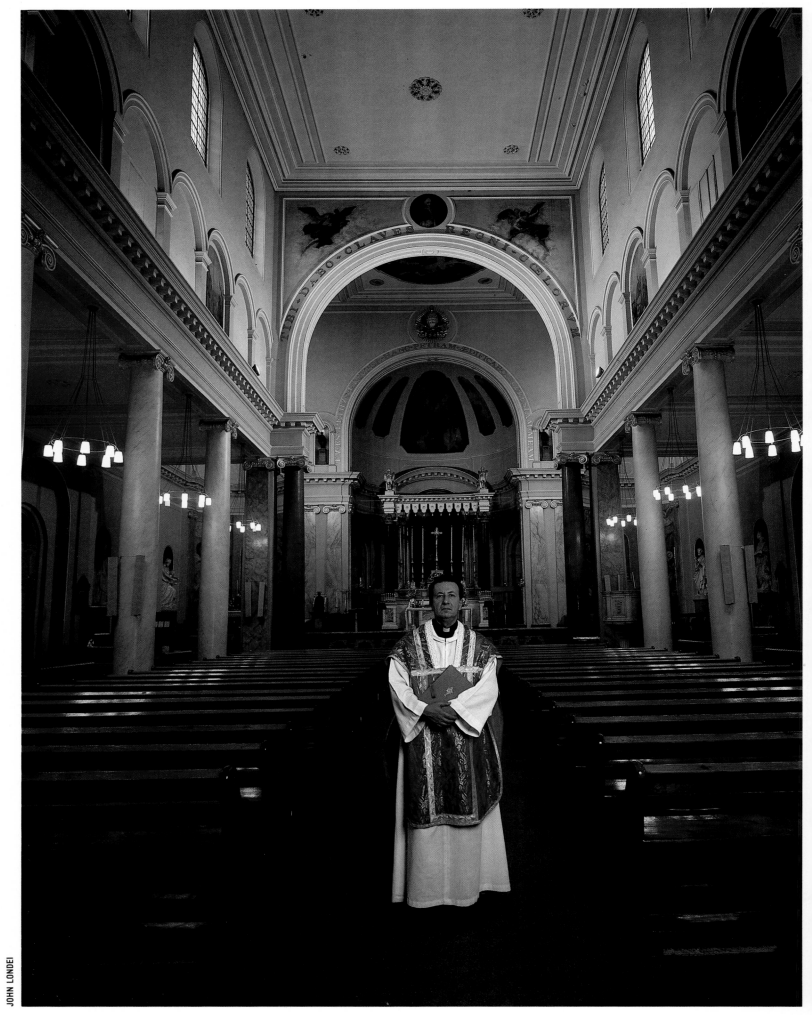

260

261

PARTY TIME

Above: Backstage at the Titantic nightclub, off Berkeley Square, two members of an act called *One Too Many* attempt to live up to their title.

Right: Lucretia (left) and her elder sister Sophie keep the jolly good fun going until all hours at the Cromwellian Club in South Kensington. Once a week in the hands of a young Lloyds broker, the Cromwellian is transformed into The Fun Club, haunt of the young county set. Lucretia and Sophie have been sent down to London from Shropshire to get a job: 'Daddy will be furious unless we get one.' Meanwhile they are living in a flat off the King's Road, and having a frightfully good time.

Following page: The Proms — Polish conductor Andrzej Panufnik conducts his own *Sinfonia Votiva*, a highly emotive work he composed in 1980 during the summer in which martial law was proclaimed in Poland. The photograph, by Laurie Lewis, was taken with a 140° Panon prototype.

LONDON SWINGS   10.45 PM

The weekly *ceili* at Quex Road Social Club, Kilburn, a night of traditional Irish music and dancing. The band, the Caravelles, are husband and wife Martin and Theresa McMahon. Martin is the Irish champion button accordion player.

Right: A lark in the bar at the Prospect Of Whitby, Wapping Wall.

Following page: Slam dancing at London's weirdest nightclub The Batcave, off Carnaby Street. Decked out like a medieval charnal house, complete with dismembered 'corpses' and lashings of synthetic blood, The Batcave caters to a horde of shaven-headed, painted ghouls of both sexes. 'Of course we were a bit wary at first,' says owner Helen Daniels of her grotesque clientele, 'but they're a lot less trouble than some of the businessmen who used to come down here with their secretaries and end up puking over everything.'

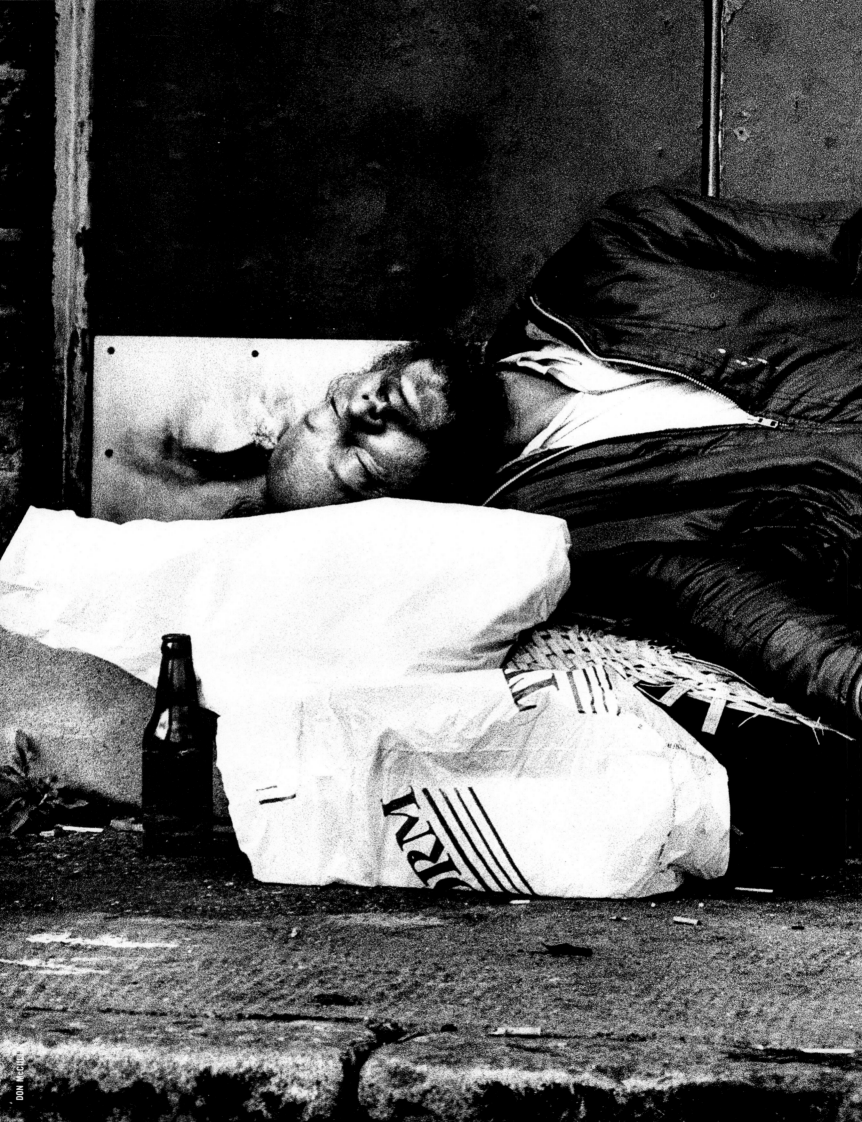

RICHARD YOUNG

FACING THE MUSIC

Princess Alexandra and her husband, Angus Ogilvy, at the Fortune Theatre with their body-guard for the evening performance. The night out at the theatre was a birthday treat for her husband from the Princess, and the press, as the royal bodyguard soon made plain to photographer Richard Young was not welcome.

Left: A birthday boy at Stringfellows nightclub receives the ultimate embarrassment — a singing telegram delivered very publicly indeed.

Previous page: Out cold in Tower Hamlets.

A NIGHT ON THE TOWN

Right: The Colony Room, Soho and artist Francis Bacon (second from right) is in earnest conversation. In the foreground owner Ian Board rests up with his injured arm.

Left: Late cabaret in Wandsworth.

CURTAIN CALL   11.30 PM

Glenda Jackson in her dressing room after the evening performance of 'Great and Small' in the Vaudeville Theatre.

Right: Quick-change artist Arturo Brachetti and singer Nicola Kimber, stars of the West End's most lavish cabaret 'Y', pose with their supporting cast after the final curtain.

Following page: 11.59 pm: The lights still burn bright in Queensway, an all-night strip catering mainly for visitors to London.

WATER STATION
ALLSOP
13
TONS
Except
for acce
TELEPHONE
LEASE FOR SALE
7777
JGP 690Y

FLAT
SEARCH

DENTAL
SURGERY

TO LE

LEASE FOR SALE

 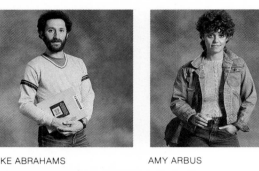   

AART AAN DE WIEL

EMILY ANDERSEN

ADRIAN BOOT

CHRISTOPHER CORMACK

    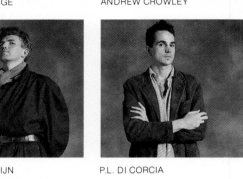

MIKE ABRAHAMS

AMY ARBUS

JANE BOWN

JOHN CLARIDGE

ANDREW CROWLEY

BARBARA BELLINGHAM

JOHN BULMER

ANTON CORBIJN

P.L. DI CORCIA

   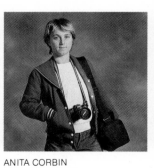 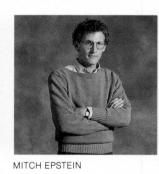

HARRY BENSON

DENNIS CALLWOOD

MATTHEW DONALDSON

  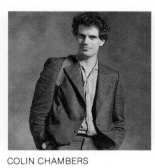  

FRANK AINSWORTH

JOHN BENTON-HARRIS

ANITA CORBIN

MITCH EPSTEIN

BRYAN ALEXANDER

ANNE BILLSON

COLIN CHAMBERS

RICK CORDELL

280

AART AAN DER WIEL
HOLLAND

Received his photographic training at college in Holland before working as an assistant in England. He works nowadays all over Europe and is recognised as an expert in car photography.

MIKE ABRAHAMS

A graduate of Polytechnic of Central London, he received a Kodak bursary in 1975 for use in photography of community development. In 1977 he photographed for *The Alienated* published by Writers and Readers. As a freelance he has contributed to a large number of newspapers, magazines etc. including The *Times, Sunday Times* and *Observer* magazines. He was co-founder in 1981 of the Network Agency.

FRANK AINSWORTH

Born in London in 1954 and became seriously interested in photography in 1979. Within the year he had left full-time employ to 'find out about the pictures'. Currently in his final year of a photography degree at The Polytechnic of Central London, he has for two years been voted as 'One of the windows to watch'. His recent work reflects a swing away from the conventional applications of the SX70 format and a move into territory more usually charted with TRI-X. Ambition: 'Not to have to steal film'.

BRYAN & CHERRY ALEXANDER

Photographers Bryan & Cherry Alexander have been working together since 1970 when they completed a 3-year photographic course at the London College of Printing. Their field of speciality is the Arctic and they have worked extensively in Northern Canada, Greenland and Lapland. Their pictures have appeared in publications in 36 countries. Among the magazines for which they have undertaken assignments are *Smithsonian, Connoisseur,* the *Observer* and *International Wildlife.* They have photographed two books for Time/ Life, *Hunters of the Polar North* (1980) and *Masked Dancers of West Africa* (1981). They live in West Sussex where they also run a photographic library that has been operating for the past 7 years.

EMILY ANDERSEN

Attended West Sussex College of Design and is a

recent graduate of the Royal College of Art. She has already received several awards, participated in two exhibitions and had her work accepted by *Event, City Limits, Guardian, Woman's Own, Photographer's Monthly, Amateur Photography* and *Cover Art Monthly.*

AMY ARBUS
USA

Is a photographer and chronicler of New York street people. Her style page *On the Street* is published monthly in the *Village Voice.* She had her first one-woman show in June 1982 at the Mudd Club in NYC. Her work has appeared in *Rolling Stone, New York Magazine* and *L'Uomo Vogue.* She is currently working on a series of photographs for *The Movies* magazine.

BARBARA BELLINGHAM

"Studied photography at the London College of Printing for three years 1969–72, in my final year specialising in editorial and photojournalism. On leaving I went to work at Thames TV as a photographic technician for 2 years. I earned enough there to buy basic equipment and a car at which point I started freelance work for women's magazines, theatre work, etc. I taught part-time at a couple of Art Colleges — Croydon College of Art and Design and Central School of Art and Design. For the past 3 years I have had my own studio and have reduced my teaching so I can concentrate on my freelance work, which ranges from still life to snapping in the streets."

HARRY BENSON

Was born in Scotland but after going to the US with the Beatles' first US tour in 1964, has remained and lives in New York with his wife Gigi and two children. His first newspaper jobs were with the *Advertiser, London Daily Sketch, Daily Express* and *Queen* magazine. In 1969 he became a contract photographer with *Life* and he works for them still. He also works for *People, New York Magazine,* French *Vogue, New York Times Magazine, Fortune* and others.
He is author of *Harry Benson on Photojournalism* published in 1982, has a most extensive list of awards including 1981 Magazine Photographer of the Year and 1982 first place in portraits division in US awards, 1983 Leica Medal of Excellence, to mention only a few. As well as he has won many British awards.

JOHN BENTON-HARRIS
USA

Born in New York City in 1939 he had his first job in a stockbroker's office on Wall Street. Then worked as photographer with Sinclair Oil Corporation, 1960–63. Studied with Alexei Brodovitch at the Design Laboratory in New York City, 1961–62. Photographer with US Army Information Office, Vicenza, Italy, 1963–65. Resident in London since 1965. Since then worked mainly as freelance photographer. Began personal view of English life in 1965, photographing London street-life. Awarded Arts Council Grants in 1974 and 1975, to document England and the English way of life. Currently involved in pursuing personal work in England and the US and teaching part-time.

ANNE BILLSON

"Born 1954 in Southport, Lancs. Studied Graphic Design at Central School of Art and Design, London. Worked as bookshop assistant, secretary, paste-up artist, cookery-book illustrator, English teacher, cinema cashier, sign writer, and lyricist for Japanese pop singers. One Gothic novel (unpublished) written while on the dole in 1978. Lived in Tokyo 1979–80. Shows of photographic work at East/ West (Tokyo, 1979), Electric Cinema (London, 1982) and Soho Poly Theatre (London, 1982).

ADRIAN BOOT

An honours graduate of Surrey University and a former physics and chemistry teacher, his long time photography interest led him to sessions with the Rolling Stones, Bob Marley and almost all rock groups of note. He has featured in most important world rock magazines and travelled regularly to the Caribbean and the USA in his work. Aside from building two of his own microcomputers has provided the photography for two books *Soul Rebel — Natural Mystic* and *Secret Policeman's Second Ball.*

JANE BOWN

Studied photography under Ifor Thomas at Guildford School of Photography. Took her first photograph (Bertrand Russell) for the *Observer* in 1950 and has been there ever since. Thames & Hudson published her book *The Gentle Eye* in 1980 and the coincidental exhibition at the National Portrait Gallery seemed to break all records. She says she is a Jane-of-all-

trades but does mostly portraits.

JOHN BULMER

Says that photography was the last of a series of childhood fascinations with things mechanical. Was thrown out of Cambridge whilst studying engineering because he spent more time on photography. He was the co-founder of *Image* the first university picture magazine and also worked on assignments at the university for both *Life* and *Queen.* He then worked at the *Express* and freelanced until joining the *Sunday Times Magazine* where he worked on the very first issue of the colour supplement.
He has travelled to over 80 countries, worked for such US publications as *Look, Holiday, Venture, Time/Life* and is actively involved in film documentaries both on still photography and direction.

DENNIS CALLWOOD
VIRGIN ISLANDS

A graduate of University of California Santa Cruz and also USCLA, Dennis resides nowadays in Los Angeles. He is a member of the Advisory Commission of the Arts 1984 Olympic Games, has held many exhibitions and his work has been exhibited on TV in Los Angeles, Japan and Mexico.

JOHN CLARIDGE

Is one of Great Britain's major advertising photographers. A Londoner, unusually for the advertising field he works on 35 mm format.

COLIN CHAMBERS

With Storm Thorgerson and Andrew Ellis he formed the design company 'Hipgnosis' which is mostly involved in the music industry, theatre, posters and record sleeves.

ANTON CORBIJN
HOLLAND

Studied photography in Holland and was assistant to a rock photographer. Then freelanced in music photography and at present is staff photographer in London for *New Musical Express.* He has photographed such people as Joe Jackson, U2, Police, etc. He says he can't stay in one place for long, doesn't like studio photography and prefers individuals to groups.

ANITA CORBIN

"Born in London, 1958. Travelled in Asia during 1977

where I began photographing people and found that a camera helped me get closer to them. Studied photography at the Polytechnic of Central London and gained a first class Honours degree in 1981 with a thesis and visual study of *Girls in Subcultures.* March 1981 got an Honorable mention in the Nikon/*Sunday Times* Young Photojournalist competition. Started freelance work in portraiture and photojournalism. Completed an M.A. in photography at the Royal College of Art in July 1983 with my main body of work on the study of the Minangkabau, a Matrilineal society of West Sumatra for which I won the *Observer* Photography prize. Member of Format Photographers."

RICK CORDELL

Says he was 'kicked out' of engineering college and then extended an amateur interest to a professional involvement in photography. Works mainly in the editorial, travel and advertising fields. Is at present working on a book on a religious festival in Sri Lanka.

CHRISTOPHER CORMACK

A member of the newly formed Impact Photos Agency. Studied photography at the London College of Printing and after working as assistant to various fashion and advertising photographers went freelance in 1977. He has worked in Europe, Africa, USA and India. His work appears in such magazines as the *Observer, Sunday Times, Sunday Telegraph, New Society, Tatler, Time, Stern,* etc.

MARIE COSINDAS
USA

A native of Boston, Marie works in large format Polaroid. Her work has appeared in *Life, Saturday Review of Literature, Newsweek, Vogue* and *Esquire* to name a few. She has participated in group showings in many countries and her work appears in many public and private collections.

ANDREW CROWLEY

Was born in Plymouth, Devon, worked for 2 years in a local studio and has been working in a London laboratory for the past year. He won the Ilford Junior Printer of the Year Award 1982.

P.L. DICORCIA
USA

Educated at the School of the

ANDREW ELLIS   STUART FRANKLIN   KEN GRIFFITHS   SUNIL JANAH

GUGLIELMO GALVIN   SUNIL GUPTA   DMITRI KASTERINE   PETER LAVERY

MISHA ERWITT   TOBY GLANVILLE   ANDRE KERTESZ   ERICA LENNARD

SALLY FEAR   CHRISTINE HANSCOMB   WILLIAM KLEIN

ANGUS FORBES   BOB GOLDEN   DAVID HURN   AKIRA KOBAYASHI   BARRY LEWIS

ARMET FRANCIS   MIKE GOLDWATER   JULIAN JOHN LEWIS

Boston Museum of Fine Arts and at Yale University, his work is featured in many collections including the Bibliotheque National, Addison Gallery of American Art, Yale University Art Gallery, Fogg Museum/Harvard University and many private collections.

MATTHEW DONALDSON

Has been a freelance assistant to many big name photographers in the advertising and fashion fields. He also spent a period in Hong Kong working on television commercials.

MITCH EPSTEIN
USA

Received his training at Rhode Island School of Design and the Cooper-Union New York. His work is now held in collections over the US, Europe and Australia. He has exhibited very widely, held public lectures, taught at Harvard University Carpenter Center for the Visual Arts and photographed for several books.

ANDREW ELLIS

See Colin Chambers

MISHA ERWITT
USA

His first published work was at age 14 — Richard Nixon's election night victory 1968. As a production technician worked on many films and TV commercials. Works as a set photographer while also fulfilling editorial assignments for very many US magazines and publications.

SALLY FEAR

Sally Fear won the first Nikon Scholarship in 1975. In 1978 Nikon sponsored an exhibition at the National Theatre of her work on *Weekend London*. Since then she has worked as a freelance photographer. Among the magazines in which her work has appeared are: the *Sunday Times* the *Observer*, *Sunday Telegraph*, *Mail on Sunday*, *Newsweek* and *Life*.

ANGUS FORBES
AUSTRALIA

Studied photography at the Royal Melbourne Institute of Technology 1962–64 before moving to London. Finally set up his own studio 'Dirty Tricks Dept' in 1973 in the area of London he fondly refers to as 'Rumpolia'.

ARMET FRANCIS
JAMAICA

Worked as an apprentice for other photographers and then became a freelance photographer specialising in fashion, advertising and reportage, mainly working for the *Sunday Times, The Africa Magazine, Gens d'Afrique, Time Out, Black Echoes*. His personal exhibitions include: The Commonwealth Institute (1974), The Jamaica High Commission (1975), Festac (1977 — Black Arts Festival in Lagos), and the British Council *Black and White* Exhibition.

STUART FRANKLIN

"Studied photography at Oxford Polytechnic and West Surrey College of Art and Design (1976–80). After leaving college I worked freelance for 1 year before joining Sygma (Paris) in May 1981.
I have worked in reportage photography for Sygma in Europe, South America, Africa and Asia."

GUGLIELMO GALVIN
IRELAND

"Worked as a builder's labourer and in various factories for a number of years, eventually ran my own processing laboratory and did little table top shots and special effect colour prints. Became part-time lecturer at London College of Printing for 7 years, then broke into editorial photography, freelancing for major national magazines like *Sunday Times Sunday*, IPC etc.

TOBY GLANVILLE

A Londoner, born in 1961, Toby Glanville worked first as a black and white processor in a West End lab and then as a photographer's assistant in North London, before setting off on his own. His focus is usually on fashion, but DITLOL, he says:
"Presented the golden opportunity to photograph everyday people in the town I will never grow tired of."

BOB GOLDEN
USA

Has been 'passionate about photography since the age of 12'. He has worked as a photojournalist for numerous magazines and publications in both the US and England where he has resided since 1971. He is presently working as a still life/food photographer and commercials director.

LYNNE GOLDSMITH
USA

Is a product of the University of Michigan. A multi-talented person she has taught school, been a publicity director, the director of late night rock show *In Concert* as well as her photography work on record sleeves for such artists as Frank Zappa, the B-52's, Simon & Garfunkel, The Village People, and others. She directs TV, produces videos, writes lyrics, even vocalises!

MIKE GOLDWATER

Born 1951, is a founding member of Network Photographers. He is a reportage photographer, widely published in the UK and Europe, at present working in the trouble spots of Central America.

KEN GRIFFITHS
NEW ZEALAND

A graduate of Canterbury University, Christchurch and also the Royal College of Art. His very successful career began with the 1971 *Telegraph* Young Photographers Award. He is retained by the *Sunday Times Magazine* which he says has enabled him to travel "and keep one step ahead of creditors" and has also worked for *Vogue, Harper's, Queen, Esquire, Life, Geo, Stern*, etc. In addition his advertising photography work reads like a *Who's Who* of world business.

HARRY GRUYAERT
BELGIUM

Born Antwerp 1941. Won Kodak Prize 1976. Published in such magazines as *Zoom* and *Photo*. Travelled extensively throughout Europe and India, is a member of the Magnum group and has numerous publications to his credit including *Double Page Monographs, Made in Belgium, Recontes Indiennes*.

SUNIL GUPTA
INDIA

Although born in New Delhi received his tertiary education in Canada, graduating B.Comm. from Concordia University, Montreal, in 1977. Received his photography training at the workshop of Philippe Halsman and the late Lisette Model. Then attended West Surrey College of Art & Design and also Royal College of Art.
Was awarded Thomas TV Travel Design Bursary 1980–81 and was a recipient (with Emily Andersen) of 3M/RCA Best Portfolio 1983. He has already a number of exhibitions to his credit and contributions to many major publications.

CHRISTINE HANSCOMB

Has worked as art director on *Vogue, Beauty in Vogue* and *Bride's Magazine*. She photographs mainly food, interiors and children, which has taken her in recent times to Europe, India and the US. Her work has appeared in leading magazines including the *Sunday Times Magazine, Good Housekeeping*, the *Observer*, as well as *Vogue* and a great variety of cookbooks.

DAVID HURN

A member of the Magnum Agency he is a very widely published photographer although self-taught. He was assistant to Michael Peto and George Varjas at Reflex Agency in London 1955–57, worked for *Observer, Life, Look, Sunday Times Magazine* in London since 1957 and in Wales since 1971. Member of Photography Committee 1972–77, Art Panel 1975–77, Arts Council of Great Britain. Head of School Documentary Photography & Film, Gwent College of Higher Education, Newport since 1973. Distinguished Visiting Artist & Adjunct Professor, Arizona State University, Tempe, 1979–80. Member Photography Committee, Council for National Academic Awards, London, since 1978.

SUNIL JANAH
INDIA

A pioneer photojournalist, his work was well known to Ghandi and Nehru. He achieved prominence from his work for 6 years throughout India recording the impact of history on his people in the 1940s and particularly the Indian tribes. He recorded the turbulent aftermath of the partition in 1947 in conjunction with his friend Margaret Bourke-White of *Life*. His collection on the women of India *The Second Chance* was published in Calcutta and his work has appeared in publications and exhibits all over the world including London, Prague, Sophia, Bucharest and Berlin. Janah has been a judge of the World Inter-Press Photo Contest and has worked for the UN, UNESCO and WHO.

DMITRI KASTERINE

Born of a White Russian father and English mother, regards himself as "self educated in the middle years. Between 1950–61 I worked as wine merchant, Lloyds Insurance broker, racing driver, airline pilot (when taking Freddie Laker's portrait at a later date, he gave me a free ticket across the Atlantic because he had worked me so hard as a pilot). In 1955 I bought a twin lens Rollie flex to use in my off-flying hours and am today still using it working on a book of portraits of writers." For the past 22 years he has worked continuously for *Harper's, Queen, Telegraph Colour Magazine, Radio Times* and many others.

ANDRE KERTESZ
HUNGARY

Was born Budapest, 1894 and by the time he moved to New York in 1936 had published, exhibited and received honours enough to fulfil most photographers' wildest ambitions. The list of his achievements is just too great to enumerate here and stretches from 1912 to the present — books, exhibitions, awards by the hundreds! The award of the Legion of Honour from the French Government in October 1983 illustrates the regard in which he is held world wide.
He is a true legend.

WILLIAM KLEIN
USA

Although born in New York 1928 has lived in Paris for a number of years. Voted by international jury at the Photokina 1963 as one of the 30 most important photographers in the history of photography. Is famous as a painter and also movie-maker and director — he wrote and directed such films as *Eldridge Cleaver, Black Panther, Muhammed Ali the Greatest, The Little Richard Story* to name only a few and his list of credits stretches back to the '50s.
He is the author of many photography books, was under contract to *Vogue* from 1955–65, his work has been taken up by all magazines of note, he has exhibited all over Europe and in the USA, has several new books under production and undoubtedly is one of the most influential forces in modern photography.

AKIRA KOBAYASHI
JAPAN

Graduated from Nikon Design School and worked as a graphic designer before becoming firstly assistant to Eisuke Shimauchi and then Elliott Erwitt. Following a stint in the US returned to Tokyo where he established his own office, Studio Show. He has held numbers of exhibitions in Japan and London. Now works from a London studio doing fashion editorial work.

LAURIE LEWIS

IAIN McKELL

SUE PACKER

O. WINSTON LINK

GERED MANKOWITZ

DAVID MONTGOMERY

RAISSA PAGE

CHRIS SCHWARZ

JOHN LONDEI

CHRIS MOYSE

JOE PARTRIDGE

NEIL SELKIRK

SANDRA LOUSADA

PETER MARLOW

MAGGIE MURRAY

JEAN PIGOZZI

PETER MARTENS

JEREMY NICHOLL

DUDLEY REED

SARITA SHARMA

EAMON McCABE

TIM MERCER

TIM O'SULLIVAN

DEREK RIDGERS

PETER LAVERY

Born Wakefield, Yorkshire. Studied at Leeds College of Art & Royal College of Art. Has worked for all major advertising agencies and was nominated for the 1983 'Top Ten Advertising Photographers'. Currently he is also working throughout Europe producing a series of photographs on the circus.

ERICA LENNARD
USA

Until two years ago Erica divided her time between Paris and New York. She has produced three books: *Sunday*; *Women, Sisters*; *Classic Gardens* and exhibited widely in Europe, UK and USA. Worked extensively in fashion, does many portraits and has featured in *Elle*, *Marie Elaine*, *Interview*, *Rolling Stone*, *Mademoiselle*, *House & Garden*, *Geo* and others.

BARRY LEWIS

A graduate in Chemistry from the University of Leicester in 1970, Barry taught science in schools for 3 years before attending the Royal College of Art. He taught photography for a year at Loughborough Art College, became a freelance photojournalist in 1976 and in 1980 was a foundation member of the Network Agency. Has held a number of exhibitions and his published work includes the books *Have Wheels, Will Travel* the story of disabled students' travel to Rome, and *Working Lives* with 5 other photographers, a contemporary history of the working class.

JULIAN JOHN-LEWIS

Is in his first year of full-time photography and received his training at Rainbow Bros and Rembrandt Bros Studios. He has already had material published in *Caribbean Times* and *Black Echoes*.

LAURIE LEWIS

Born in London 1944. Attended Walthamstow Art School, Royal College and UCLA Film Schools. He now freelances in film and photography.

O. WINSTON LINK
USA

Has been a photographer for over 50 years and is Manhattan based, working mainly in the industrial field. His work in the '50s recording the last steam-powered railroad in action — the Norfolk and Western — has been widely publicised and has won several awards.

JOHN LONDEI
CANADA

Born in Montreal, he was raised in Southwick near Brighton. Worked as an insurance clerk for 4 years but says he escaped thanks to Norman Tudgay of Medway College of Art who took him in when really he lacked sufficient entrance qualifications.
Now based in London he works mainly in advertising using large format cameras.

SANDRA LOUSADA

Studied photography at London Polytechnic. After period as 'dogsbody' and assistant at several studios went freelance at age 21. Worked with English Stage Company at Royal Court in the '60s. Began shooting for *Queen* when David Hamilton was art director and through '70s shot fashion and beauty for most London magazines. Photographed for *Conde Nast* in the US, developed her 'children' photography.

EAMON McCABE

After doing a film course in 1969 in San Francisco, returned to London. Following a spell as a stills photographer and dabbling in 'shooting pop' settled on sport as his first love. Worked on local newspapers and the *Guardian* and has now been with the *Observer* for 6 years. Held an exhibition at Walker Art Gallery, Liverpool, 1982, has won Sports Photographer of the Year three times and this year is one of the judges!

DON McCULLIN

Born in London he is one of the world's best known and most accomplished photojournalists. He has received dozens of awards including International press Photographer of the Year many times. Has published four books, *The Destruction Business*, *Don McCullin*, *The Palestinians*, *Beirut*. He is probably most famous for his war coverage and has been twice seriously wounded in the course of his work.

IAIN McKELL

From 1974–78 he studied graphic design at Exeter College of Art. He is a freelance, mainly editorial, whose work appears in such publications as *Observer Supplement*, *Sunday Express*, English *Vogue*, *The Face*, *Time Out*, Italian *Lei* and others.

GERED MANKOWITZ

Has been working as a professional photographer in London since 1963. He is renowned for his work on several hundred record sleeves but is also a most active advertising and editorial photographer.

PETER MARLOW

Born 1952 in England. Took up photography after leaving Manchester University having graduated with psychology degree. Began work as photographer in 1975 — worked as a cruise line photographer for nine months and saved enough money to make an extended trip photographing round South America.
The pictures from that trip were used in *New York Times* magazine. From that exposure he was offered retainer from Sygma. Joined Magnum in 1980 — has since been working regularly for various magazines *Newsweek*, *Sunday Times*, *Paris Match*, etc. He was one of the team flown out specially to photograph *A Day in the Life of New Zealand*.

PETER MARTENS
HOLLAND

Born Rotterdam 1937, graduated from Dutch School of Photography in The Hague. First worked as movie stills photographer. Is a freelance principally featured in *Panorama* magazines. Has held exhibitions throughout Europe and had many essays published on a great variety of subjects as well as two books *250 on 8* and *Nothing Special*.

TIM MERCER

Personal assistant to Professor John Hedgecoe for five years and then was a student in photography at the Royal College of Art. He has worked for the past 8 years as a freelance photographer for such publications as the *Sunday Times* and *Sunday Telegraph*; *Harper's*, *Queen*, *Now*, *Tatler*, *FBA*, *Zeit* and *Observer* magazines.

DAVID MONTGOMERY
USA

Although born in Brooklyn he has been a resident of the UK for 23 years. Commenced as a fashion photographer for *Queen* magazine and his work now appears in most publications of note — *Sunday Times*, *Vogue*, *Tatler*, *Esquire*, *Rolling Stone*, *Fortune* and *New York Times*. He is an extremely versatile photographer covering portraiture, fashion, advertising, still life and editorial.

CHRIS MOYSE

Born in Manchester 1949. First camera bought while hitch-hiking round USA. First published work, postcards in Belize, South America. Returned to London working as a freelance. Published book on boxing — *The Hardest Game* with Harry Carpenter 1981. Now working in London for *New Society* and *Vogue*. After his 24 hours on London's underground reckons he'll need a year's break before he rides the tube again!

MAGGIE MURRAY

Has travelled extensively in Africa, India and Europe working on commissions for development agencies and educational publishers. Was a collaborator on two books *Photography Guidelines* and *Our Own Freedom*.
She is a member of the Format Agency and is working on a grant-aided book on women and unemployment in Oxford.

JEREMY NICHOLL
IRELAND

Jeremy has led a varied career but settled finally for photography. Having started with an old Praktika his success has enabled him to buy some 'decent' cameras. His news and current affairs pictures appear most regularly in the *Sunday Times* and most national papers and he has contributed to *Time*, *Newsweek*, *Economist* and *Der Spiegel*.

TIM O'SULLIVAN

'After an Arts Foundation course I spent three years at London College of Printing studying photography and a further 1½ years assisting various advertising and fashion photographers. I ceased being an assistant because of what, not who I knew, and started as an unknown yet aspiring photographer seven months ago.

SUE PACKER

Is a graduate of Newport College of Art and the Royal College of Art. 1979 won the *Observer* photography prize, 1981 started as freelance and has contributed to the *Times*, *Observer*, *Telegraph*, *Cosmopolitan*, *Good Housekeeping*, and *Over 21*.

RAISSA PAGE
CANADA

Raissa Page is an ex-patriate Canadian who has been living and working in London since 1959. Five years ago she abandoned a successful career in social welfare to work full-time as a photojournalist. Her searing coverage of daily life in long term hospitals for the mentally handicapped brought her first major recognition as a 'young' photographer.
Her work has appeared in a number of leading newspapers and magazines. She was a contributor to the touring exhibition *Restricted Practices — Documentary Photography in Britain 1982*. More recently she has been working as a member of the Format Agency.

JOE PARTRIDGE

Writes and broadcasts regularly on photography. ITV feature his networked programme 'Me and My Camera' from which two best selling books have also been produced. He writes a column for *Camera Weekly* and is an occasional contributor to many other magazines.

JEAN PIGOZZI
FRANCE

Lives in Switzerland and is a Harvard graduate. He has had shows in Paris, New York, Tel Aviv, authored *Pigozzi's Journal of the Seventies* published by Doubleday and is an extensive contributor to *Rolling Stone* magazine.

DUDLEY REED

Attended London School of Art and London Film School. Whilst working for Bookbinder trained in still life photography. He is under contract to *Conde Nast*, works for *Tatler*, *American Vogue*, *Vanity Fayre* and is an editorial and portraits specialist.

DEREK RIDGERS

Is widely known for his work on the popular youth culture. Having studied advertising and marketing he was an art director with an advertising agency for 10 years before devoting himself full time to photography. He does a lot of street, night club and pop star portraits, has held four one-man shows and his work is to be found in such publications as *The Face*, and *Photo*.

RED SAUNDERS

Started as 'tea-boy, keen young lad' in various studios before becoming a freelance in 1966. Has a mixed client list, works on all formats with a personal bias to 'mixed

STAK STEVE TYNAN ERIC WATSON PAUL WINDSOR

JOHN STURROCK HORST WACKERBARTH DENIS WAUGH SUSAN WITNEY

PENNIE SMITH GERAY SWEENEY ED WHITE

HOMER SYKES RICHARD WAITE WIL WHITE IAN YEOMANS

SALLY SOAMES PIERRE TOUTAIN CALVIN WALKER JERRY YOUNG

TOBY GLANVILLE

LAURIE SPARHAM TESSA TRAEGER VAL WILMER RICHARD YOUNG

286

light' portraits both formal and surreal. He was one of the photographers flown out to photograph *A Day In The Life of New Zealand*.

CHRIS SCHWARZ

Works as a freelance in London having started photography 'by accident' in 1970 in Japan. Group and solo exhibitions have included *Inside Whitechapel* at Whitechapel Art Gallery; *The E.Z. Festival* an exhibition of homelessness at the G L C.; *The Quality of Life* for the opening of the National Theatre; *The People of Darlington*; *Seven Dancers* and also *Our Neighbours* for Riverside Studios; *London Calling* a touring exhibition highlighting the problems of young people arriving in the capital and for which he received a G L C. award.

NEIL SELKIRK

Born in London and studied at London College of Printing. Went to New York in 1970 where he now resides. He worked for Avedon and Hiro and now does mostly editorial and advertising photography.

SYD SHELTON

Although born in Yorkshire he lives now in Australia. He has both studied and taught art in the UK and Australia, conducted a successful design and photography studio in London and contributed his photography to many major magazines. Has worked on a number of books and most recently was the designer of *A Day in the Life of New Zealand*.

SARITA SHARMA
UGANDA

Born in 1959 in Kampala she moved to England as an exile. Photographer Julian Cowan awakened her interest in photography following a trip to Mexico. Says "Through photography I want to show that Indian women can be as independent as they wish."

PENNIE SMITH

Attended the Twickenham College of Technology and after a stint on *Frendz* magazine she moved to *New Musical Express* as staff photographer. Has held exhibitions at Institute of Contemporary Art and Battersea Arts Centre. 1981 published her book *The Clash*.

SALLY SOAMES

Her first professional assignment was for the *Observer* in 1963. After contributing to

the *Guardian*, British and American film and television companies, international magazines etc. she joined the *Sunday Times* in 1968. She covered the Yom Kippur war in 1973 and worked in Israel for 2 years. Has contributed to many exhibitions and her most recent was of photographs taken in Auschwitz shown at the Jewish Museum in New York.

LAURIE SPARHAM

A founder member of the Network group, Laurie worked previously with the Report Agency. His work appears regularly in newspapers, magazines and journals in the UK.

STAK
CYPRUS

Studied at the London College of Printing but entered the family wholesale and manufacturing business in materials and cloths. He then turned to photography and has been a 'major' in the advertising field for 11 years.

JOHN STURROCK

After studying physics at Leicester University decided his interest was really photography. He is particularly noted for his work in the socio-political field and is featured regularly in the *Socialist Worker*, newspapers and such magazines as *Newsweek*, and *Economist*.

GERAY SWEENEY
IRELAND

Attended the foundation course of the Derby College of Art before studying for three years at the Guildford School of Art, where she says the best part was a leaving party! She returned to freelance in Belfast in 1969 but then moved to London in 1981 and is perhaps best known for her work *Cures* on ancient and modern herbal treatments.

HOMER SYKES
CANADA

Born in Vancouver he attended London College of Printing 1968–70. Homer is a freelance who has worked with Woodfin Camp in the US and also with Viva photographic agency in France. He has a number of exhibitions to his credit as well as several books — *Once a Year* on traditional country customs published by Gordon Fraser and *Facts About a Pop Group*, featuring Paul McCartney & Wings, of which Homer was co-author.

PIERRE TOUTAIN
FRANCE

Born in Normandy but lives in Paris. He has been travelling throughout Europe, Asia and North Africa working as a freelance and under contract to major international magazines.
He is best know for his coverage of the Poland Crisis, Vietnam and Kampuchea.

TESSA TRAEGER

Studied large format camera at Guildford School of Art. She is particularly known for still life work on food and flowers and works out of a studio in Chelsea and also a barn on her farm in Devon. Works principally in advertising and editorial in Paris, Milan, London and New York. She has had two books published from her *Vogue* work on food.

STEVE TYNAN

Born in Manchester 1960, he studied at Bournemouth College of Art and the Pratt Institute, New York. Works for *Face, Sunday Times*, and others. Classes himself as mainly an editorial photographer.

HORST WACKERBATH
GERMANY

Resident these days in Los Angeles he has photographed for all major advertising agencies in the USA and Europe. His work has frequently appeared in such publications as *Life, Stern, Vogue, Playboy* and *Zoom*. Most recently his exhibition featuring a red couch in numerous unexpected situations and locations shows him to have a most whimsical and imaginative approach.

RICHARD WAITE

Attended Bristol College of Art and Design and also Bournemouth & Poole College of Art and Design. He received a South East Arts bursary in 1977 when he also held travelling exhibitions. From 1978–80 he was a freelance assistant at the Association of Fashion Advertising and Editorial Photographers since when he has been an editorial photographer of location and architectural interiors as well as portraiture.

CALVIN WALKER
JAMAICA

Although he lived in London for many years, at present works in Paris as a fashion

and beauty photographer. He has ambitions of working later in cinematography.

ERIC WATSON

Born 1955 in Newcastle upon Tyne to a family of shipbuilders and miners, he graduated from the Hornsey College of Art. Works for many magazines and record companies, photographs for numbers of record sleeves as well as editorial work. *Smash Hits* regularly feature his photography.

DENIS WAUGH
NEW ZEALAND

Was born in Dunedin, New Zealand. Arrived in U K 1967 for projected short stay. After working briefly in London art photographic studio attended the new still photography course at Royal College of Art. Has freelanced ever since. Clients now include major advertising agencies in London and abroad, magazines such as *Express, Life, Fortune, Geo, Smithsonian, Connoiseur, New York, Times Supplement, Sunday Times, Observer, Sunday, Good Housekeeping*, as well as special photography on feature films.

ED WHITE

Born 1949 in Surrey, studied at London College of Printing 1969–72 and has worked in advertising ever since. Recently sold his studio to concentrate on outdoor location work specialising in 8 × 10 format.

WILL WHITE

Attended Southampton College of Art and West Surrey College of Art. '. . . did odd jobs in America, scaffolder in Germany.' Now works as assistant in Rembrandt Bros Studio in London. Other interests are illustration and painting.

VAL WILMER

Was born in Yorkshire, England, in 1941 and grew up in London. In 1973 the Victoria and Albert Museum, London held a show of her photographs of Afro-American musicians. Three years later, her book based on the exhibition *The Face of Black Music* was published in New York. She is the author of two other books about black music, *Jazz People* and *As Serious as Your Life*, and her photographs formed the basis for the film *Jazz is Our Religion*. She is a member of Britain's first all-women photo agency, Format.

PAUL WINDSOR

Has not only been recognised for his photography for very many years but also as an advertising art director and for his involvement with television commercials.

SUSAN WITNEY

Studied at Medway College of Design and Maidstone College of Art. As well as several teaching jobs she has found time to exhibit and publish — *British Journal of Photography* and *Vogue*. She received the *Vogue* Award for Photography June 1983.

IAN YEOMANS

Worked as an assistant in a fashion studio 1957–62 before becoming staff photographer for *Queen* magazine. Following a period of 5 years as staff photographer for *Sunday Times Magazine* set out as a freelance which he has remained most successfully.

JERRY YOUNG

Born 1946. Started working life as an electrical engineer. Changed over to photographer in 1975 working out of London mostly in editorial with some company report work. Specialises in adventure sports and flying. A book on hot air ballooning was published in 1980. His work has appeared in *Life, Business Week, Stern, Smithsonian, Le Figaro, Sunday Telegraph* and many others.

RICHARD YOUNG

"Born London 1947. Left school at 15 and worked in retail clothing until 23. Lived in New York for 5 years during which spent 2 years in Jimmy Hendrix's recording studio. Also did a spot of window dressing in several big stores.
Returned to London and worked in a bookshop where the boss gave me a camera to obtain photographs for a book — the result was useless but I kept the camera and became proficient. Really fell into photography and today work for *Daily Express* and have work syndicated world wide. Am best described as a paparazzi photographer."

Contributors

Bill Green.	Colin Still.
Jo Anderson.	Leon Morris.
Steve Harper.	Chris Davies.

Following page: Big Ben, under repair, at the stroke of midnight.

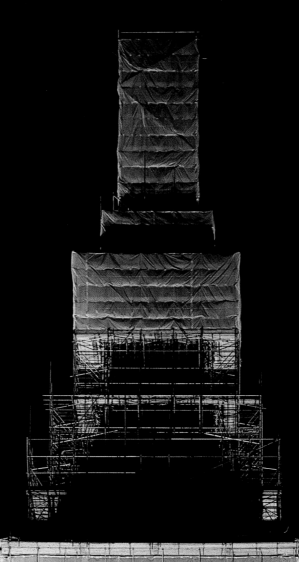
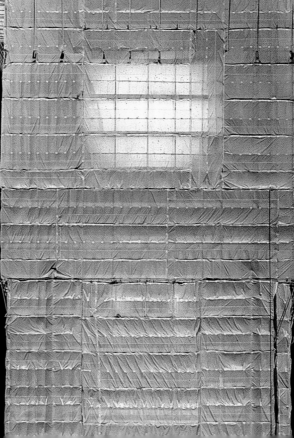

We gratefully acknowledge the assistance of the following

CETA CETA COLOUR LABORATORIES LTD

ftp FTP PHOTOPRINTS LTD

KJP KEITH JOHNSON PHOTOGRAPHICS LTD

Canon CANON CAMERAS (UK) LTD

Nikon NIKON CAMERAS (UK) LTD

GLC GREATER LONDON COUNCIL

ilea INNER LONDON EDUCATION AUTHORITY

Phoenix PHOENIX DESPATCH RIDERS

LONDON TRANSPORT

RADIO TAXICABS LTD

ILFORD ILFORD PHOTOGRAPHIC LTD

AFAEP THE ASSOCIATION OF FASHION ADVERTISING & EDITORIAL PHOTOGRAPHERS

ED WHITE